Irish Food & Folklore

Irish Food & Folklore

A guide to the cooking, myths and history of Ireland

Clare Connery

Bounty
Books

NOTES

Both metric and imperial measures have been given in all recipes. Use one set of measurements only and not a mixture of both.

Standard level spoon measurements are used in all recipes:
1 tablespoon = one 15 ml spoon
1 teaspoon = one 5 ml spoon

Eggs should be medium unless otherwise stated.

Milk should be full fat unless otherwise stated.

Pepper should be freshly ground unless otherwise stated.

Fresh herbs should be used unless otherwise stated. If unavailable use dried herbs as an alternative but halve the given quantities.

Ovens should be preheated to the specified temperature – if using a fan assisted oven, follow the manufacturer's instructions for adjusting the time and temperature.

Publishing Director: Laura Bamford
Commissioning Editor: Nicola Hill
Senior Editor: Sasha Judelson
Assistant Editor: Catharine Davey
Art Director: Keith Martin
Senior Designer: Louise Leffler
Designer: Les Needham
Picture Researcher: Claire Gouldstone
Production Controller: Phillip Chamberlain

Acknowledgements

Bill Doyle : front cover, bottom, 1, 3, 5, 7, 8, 9, 10, 11, 12, 22, 34, 36, 49, 56, 66, 76, 85, 94, 97, 104, 106, 112, 117, 120, 132, 136, 139
Octopus Publishing Group Ltd./Christopher Hill : 15, 18, 27, 31, 35, 39, 43, 47, 50, 55, 59, 62, 67, 71, 75, 79, 82, 87, 91, 95, 98, 103, 107, 111, 114, 119, 123, 127, 131, 135, 138
R.S. Magowan : 28, 40, 58, 92
Alan Newnham : Front jacket inset

First published by Hamlyn, a division of Octopus Publishing Group, in 1997.

This 2001 edition published by Chancellor Press, an imprint of Bounty Books, a division of Octopus Publishing Group Ltd, 2-4 Heron Quays, London E14 4JP
Reprinted 2004, 2006, 2007
Copyright © 1997 Octopus Publishing Group Limited

ISBN-13: 978-0-753709-68-9
ISBN-10: 0-753709-68-6

A CIP catalogue record of this book is available from the British Library

Produced by Toppan, Hong Kong

Printed and bound in China

Contents

introduction

Ireland is a beguiling and charming land with a culture steeped in myth and legend, fairy tale and folklore. The very breath of the wind in the trees, the babbling of the water in the stream, the lowing of the cattle in the deep green pastures and the crackling of the fire in the hearth all draw us into Ireland's mysterious past. Its foods, feasts and festivals are linked to the timeless rural calendar and the changing seasons of the year. Here the past is evoked and the spirits of Ireland, with the bounty from the land, sea and shore, are laid before you in words and pictures.

Myth and legend, fact and fiction are inextricably intertwined within the psyche of Ireland. Cultural traditions and the folklore of the past are never too far from the surface and still carry weight, even if only in superstition. In what is still largely an agricultural country, the pattern of everyday life is bound to the vagaries of nature and many of the festivals and rituals are closely associated with the changing seasons.

This is not to say that Ireland is unsophisticated. In every technical sense she is a modern nation. However, in spite of this, there is still a fascination with the past, in particular for a period which spanned a thousand years, from about 500 BC. During this time, the richness of the Celtic culture, with its highly developed religion and sophisticated law system, was the creative force. Celtic scholarship and knowledge, was, for many centuries, passed on orally, rather than written down, the spoken word was therefore all powerful. The beliefs, codes of behaviour, social systems, folklore, myths, legends, poetry and song, which bound the people together, giving them a sense of continuity and identity, were entrusted to an elite of druids (philosophers), seers (prophets) and bards (lyric poets), who preserved this unique body of knowledge through the oral tradition. It was not until the 7th century AD that the myths and stories of Celtic culture were written down by monastic scribes. Such tales portray a tribal and rural society of gods and goddesses, warrior princes of major and minor kingdoms, battles, cattle raids, feasting, fertility and heroism.

IRISH MYTH AND LEGEND

Irish mythology is, in essence, heroic. Colossal figures, endowed with magical powers, dominate. The Tuatha de Danaan (the people of the goddess Dana) were the god-like rulers of the pre-Christian Irish, imbued with superhuman traits. Dagda was their leader. He possessed two implements with magical powers. A gigantic club, one end of which could slay enemies, whilst the other could heal the sick. He also had a huge cauldron, large enough to contain food for a whole tribe, a testament to his own enormous appetite. At the mythical battle of Magh Tuireadh, his enemies filled the cauldron with a gargantuan stew of goat, sheep, swine, meal and fat. Dagda was forced to eat the stew, using his huge ladle (big enough to hold a man and a woman). He triumphed, consuming the stew with ease. This epic tale covers many of the recurrent themes of Irish mythology and folklore, typically dealing with fertility, plenty and victory over all enemies, including hunger.

Eventually the Tuatha de Danaan were defeated by invaders and scattered and shrank in both size and importance. This diminishing of stature was reinforced by the early Christian scribes who were more inclined to accept the elevation to heroic status of mythical, larger than life characters rather than gods. As W. B. Yeats stated in *The Book of Fairy and Folk Tales of Ireland*, 'the pagan heroes grew bigger and bigger until they turned into giants'.

The two most renowned of the heroes in Irish folklore are Cúchalainn, reputedly the son of the God Lugh, and Fionn MacCumhail (Finn Mac Cool). These are the principal participants of the most famous Irish cycles the *Ulster* or *Red Branch Cycle* and the *Fenian Cycle*. The former is the greatest of all Irish sagas, and the most famous story in the cycle, that of the Tain Bó Cuailgne (The Cattle Raid of Cooley) tells of how Medb (Maeve) the much married Queen of Connacht, through envy of her husband's possessions, leads an army to capture the famous Brown Bull of Cuailgne. Cúchulainn, the champion warrior of all Ireland defends Ulster single handed against Medb's forces. This revered warrior, who does not fear death, is also the central figure in another epic saga *The Champion's Portion*, also known as *Bricriu's Feast* – where food plays a significant role, the 'champion's portion' being the reward for the undisputed champion. At Bricriu's Feast, the 'champion's portion' as

described by Frank Delaney in *Legends of the Celts* contains: 'a seven year old boar, ripe and sweet, which, since it was born, had been fed only on sweetened porridge, oatmeal, fresh milk, nuts, wheat, meat and broth, according to the seasons. In addition he had a

cow, seven years old too, who, since birth had been fed only heather, herbs, corn and sweet meadow grass. And to accompany this cauldron full of wine, pig meat and beef, one hundred wheat cakes had been cooked in honey using a bushel of wheat to every four cakes.'

Because Cúchulainn's status as champion is questioned by rival warriors, a long series of physical trials is instigated against these

pretenders. Meanwhile, the feasting continues while Cúchulainn establishes his supremacy, before returning to claim the 'champion's portion'.

Almost equal in status to the figure of Cúchulainn is Fionn MacCumhail, the most celebrated leader of the

Fianna (The Royal Bodyguard of the High Kings), who, as a young man, was the pupil of Finegas, a druid poet. Finegas had for many years sought to catch the 'Salmon of Knowledge', a red spotted fish, which acquired its knowledge by eating the berries of the rowan as they fell into the water. When eventually he succeeds, Finegas gives the fish to Fionn to cook, who in doing so burns his fingers on the fish and acquires wisdom.

As with Cúchulainn, Fionn has many physical and mystical adventures, including his defeat of Daire Dawn (King of the World). His unrequited love for Grainne and his pursuit of herself and Diarmuid, her lover, is a classic love epic.

FAIRIES AND FOLKLORE

The legends and stories of Ireland are not only peopled with heroic warriors and mystical gods but are filled with strange and intriguing tales of 'little people', with the power to enchant, befuddle and outwit human kind. Historical research explains these tales of 'little people' as the literal shrinking of the pagan gods of Ireland on the arrival of Christianity. From this time, the gods lost their religious significance, receding into legend and fairy tale, but retaining magical powers in the imagination of the people.

The Irish word for fairy is *sidheóg* which comes from the description of the old Irish gods who were relegated to fairy status as *aés sídhe* - 'the people of the hills'. Intimately associated with rural life, they are reputed to be swift to bless and quick to anger, thus symbolising a combination of good and evil, both harbingers of fortune and misfortune. They must therefore be respected and placated. The tradition of leaving crumbs from the evening meal by the hearth, a saucer of milk on the bedroom windowsill and glowing embers in the fire place as a welcome, are the most homely examples.

The fairies can be divided into two principal groups, trooping fairies and solitary fairies. The trooping fairies are usually dressed in green and are mostly friendly; blessed with the power of healing, they help people in trouble. The solitary fairies are dressed in red, prefer their own company and cause mischief. Some of the more important solitary fairies are:

THE LEPRECHAUN (*Leith Bhrogan*) who is in fact the god Lugh, who was driven underground with the other gods and whose image was diminished in popular folklore into a fairy craftsman, a shoemaker or tailor. He is somewhat ill-tempered and possesses a crock of gold, to be given to whoever catches him.

THE POOKA (*Púca*) is a malevolent fairy, capable of assuming any shape, usually animal, and is particularly troublesome to travellers, who may unwittingly jump on his back when the pooka takes the shape of a horse.

THE BANSHEE (*Bean Sidhé*) is a 'woman of the hills' (also known as the 'lady of death'), who attaches herself to a family and warns of approaching death by emitting an eerie wailing and crying. The banshee is sometimes seen accompanied by the coach-a-bower, a funeral carriage drawn by a headless horse and driven by the headless Dallahan.

Music has always served as a foundation stone to the

cultural life of Ireland. It therefore seems fitting that fairy music should be a central source for the powers of the 'little people'. Legend tells of magical music capable of healing the sick and inspiring great men, but also of enchanting young children away from the mortal world and into fairy land; a changeling child is left by the fairies in the place of the mortal baby.

Come away! O, human child!
To the woods and waters wild
With a fairy hand in hand,
For the world's more full of
Weeping than you can understand
(W B Yeats, 'The Stolen Child')

Tir-na-N-og or *Tir-inna-Beo* means 'Country of the Young' or 'Land of the Living' and is the fairy land of Irish mythology. It is often interpreted as symbolising the afterlife, a heavenly land which you can only reach by journeying. On this mythical isle neither death nor old age exist and the inhabitants know neither pain nor sadness.

FEASTS AND FESTIVALS

Mythical folk, whether the larger than life characters of heroic legend, or the fairies of the fields, are noted for their appetite for food and in this respect they are no different from the mortals who toil to produce their sustenance from the countryside.

Four great seasonal pagan Celtic festivals are recorded in mythical tradition, all associated with the farming year – Imbolic (February), Beltaine (May), Lughnasa (August) and Samhain (November). Each of these quarters had its own specific activities and celebrations influenced not only by pastoral and arable traditions but by pagan and Christian legend and folklore.

Imbolic

The start of the year in Ireland's rural calendar is the Imbolic festival (February), the beginning of spring. This was linked with the cult of Brigid, daughter of Dagda, a

multi-functional goddess who protected women in childbirth, presided over the ale harvest and was also associated with milk and butter-making, poetry and property. She retained many of her pagan roles even when she was adopted as a saint by the Christian church.

It was said that on St Brigid's day the saint placed her foot in the water and warmed it, giving rise to the belief that from that time on the weather should improve, spring ploughing could begin and milk and butter production increase. On St Brigid's eve rushes were fashioned into protective charms known as Brigid's crosses to protect the house and the livestock from harm and from fire. Milk and butter were particularly susceptible to supernatural influences and for that reason the first rich milk given by a newly calved cow, called 'beastlings', was poured on the roots of fairy thorn trees to appease the 'little people'. When the butter was made a small ball of it was smeared or tossed on top of the dresser as an offering to the fairies.

On the coast the spring tide closest to the festival was believed to be the greatest of the year, and so it became the time when the people gathered seaweed to fertilize their crops and collected shellfish and other produce of the shore. In some parts of the country a limpet or periwinkle was placed at the four corners of the house to bring good luck to the fishermen and draw a bountiful harvest from the sea. There were celebrations in the house too and a special festive supper prepared. Flummery, a type of oatmeal blancmange, and sowans, an oatmeal drink, along with apple cake, apple dumplings and a fruit bread called barm brac, butter, freshly churned that day, and buttermilk, were served. The main dishes ranged from colcannon – mashed potatoes with spring onions and shredded cabbage – to fowl, bacon and sometimes mutton. It was also customary to give gifts of butter, buttermilk or pieces of meat to poor neighbours. Indeed, pieces of bread and butter, a cake or dish of porridge were often left out for St Brigid herself.

Beltaine

The next major festival in the rural calendar is the Gaelic Beltaine, the feast of the fires of 'Bel' (Bilé, the God of life and death). This falls at the beginning of May, to celebrate the beginning of summer and triumph over the dark powers. Many superstitions were associated with May Day, particularly those connected with the supernatural world. Witches and fairies were thought to be active and precautions were taken to ward off their evil intentions.

Not only were wells, fields, byres and houses guarded, but on May eve bonfires were lit and both men and women leapt over the flames before driving their cattle through smouldering ashes or between two small fires to protect them from evil spells. Milk was poured on the threshold of the house and around fairy thorn trees. May flowers were crushed to provide a juice which was then used to wash the cows' udders. Sometimes the cows' backs were marked with the sign of a cross and, after milking on May Day, a cross was made with the froth from the milk. A bunch of primroses was tied to each cow's tail to protect it against malevolent fairies. A sprig of rowan was also thought to protect against evil and was hung on the byre door, on the milk pail or on the cow's horns. Sometimes, not even

rowan offered protection against the butter stealing fairies and, as a result, no milk was given away on May Day and no stranger was allowed to milk the cows. A small quantity of the butter which was made on this day was kept in the dairy for the rest of the season.

Lughnasa

The beginning of harvest was marked by the festival of Lughnasa on 1 August, a druidic festival, held in honour of the god Lugh, to ensure that the corn was safely gathered in. Corn dollies were formed out of the last sheaf to be cut and it was customary for the first flour ground from the harvest to be made into a loaf of bread and porridge. When the corn was gathered, it was time for the harvest of the hedges and

orchards. Blackberries, whortleberries, blaeberries (billberries), wild raspberries and strawberries were collected, along with the sacred apples. Finally, nuts were gathered and stored, particularly the hazelnut, which, when grown by a stream, was believed to represent kernels of wisdom. Christianity adapted this feast and named it Lammas (Feast of the First Fruits).

Samhain

Many of these feasts and celebrations pale into insignificance when compared to the festival of Samhain which marks the dying, or end, of the rural year on All-Hallows Eve, 31 October, better known now as Hallowe'en. It was an intensely spiritual time for it was then that the 'other world' became visible to mankind and when spiritual forces were let loose on the human world. At Hallowe'en it is believed that the spirits and ghosts set out to wreak vengeance on the living. It was thought to be unlucky not to make preparations for the return of the dead, so the door of the house was left open, seats set around the fire and sowans left ready for the spirits.

The crops should, by now, have all been gathered in. No fruits were picked after this time, for, it was thought, that the Pooka was busy destroying them by spitting on

them. The animals were brought in from their summer pastures, some were slaughtered and some kept for breeding. It was a time for family celebrations, markets, fairs and feasts and there are many foods associated with the occasion.

The vigil of the Feast of All Saints has for many centuries been a day of abstinence, so meat was not generally eaten. However, there were many other traditional dishes to compensate, using the produce of the harvest – apple cake, potato apple cake, boxty pancakes, bread and dumplings, potato puddings and colcannon, barm brack, oatcakes, batter pancakes and blackberry pies in addition to apples and nuts – all were favourites of this season.

No matter what the dish

chosen, it was thought to bring luck if a wedding ring and other charms were baked inside it. This would decide the destiny, during the coming year, of the person finding it on their plate.

Through all the changing seasons of the year, with their associated foods and customs, there is not only a vital relationship between man, his animals, his crops and the countryside, but a constant and unbroken link with the past. Although the myths, legends and fairy stories of Ireland's heroic and mystical past may seem to have small relevance in today's sophisticated society, they do still have the power to inspire and entertain, comfort and sustain. After all, the past lives on in our minds, in our landscape and the dishes we take to our table.

soups

Soup has always been important in the Irish diet. It was often served at every meal or as the basis of the meal itself, when it was so thick and rich with meat, vegetables and potatoes, that it was called an 'atin and drinkin' soup. Soups were made from whatever ingredients were available, wild herbs, vegetables, seeds, nuts and grains, along with meat, fish, shellfish, game and poultry. One of the earliest soups was made from ground oatmeal, boiled in water, with chopped vegetables. When meat was added to it, it was referred to as broth.

Purée of Potato Soup with Bacon & Chives

50 g/2 oz butter

1 large onion, roughly chopped

750 g/1½ lb potatoes, peeled and roughly chopped

750 ml/1¼ pints chicken stock

750 ml/1¼ pints milk

50 ml/2 fl oz single cream

6 rashers streaky bacon, derinded, chopped and crisply fried

salt and pepper

1 tablespoon snipped chives, to garnish

Melt the butter in a large saucepan and fry the onion until soft, without colouring. Add the potatoes, stock, milk and season with salt and pepper. Bring to the boil, then reduce the heat and simmer for 40–45 minutes, stirring occasionally to prevent the potatoes from sticking.

Purée the soup in a liquidizer or food processor until smooth. Return to the pan, taste and adjust the seasoning if necessary and stir in the cream and bacon. Bring to the boil and serve in individual soup bowls garnished with snipped chives.

COOK'S NOTES
Water can be used instead of chicken stock but the result will be much less flavoursome. Vegetable stock, even from a cube, would be preferable.

Serves 6–8
Preparation time: 15–20 minutes
Cooking time: 45–50 minutes

They make the blood warmer,

You'll feel like a farmer,

For this is every cook's opinion,

No savoury dish without an onion.

(JONATHAN SWIFT)

Leek & Potato Soup

25 g/1 oz butter

2 large leeks, finely sliced

250 g/8 oz potatoes, roughly diced

1 onion, roughly chopped

750 ml/1¼ pints chicken stock or water

300 ml/½ pint milk

salt and pepper

1 tablespoon snipped chives, to garnish

Melt the butter in a large saucepan, add the leeks, potatoes and onion. Stir well to coat with the butter. Cover tightly with a piece of greaseproof paper and cook over a very gentle heat for about 15 minutes until softening, stirring frequently to prevent the vegetables from colouring.

Add the stock or water and milk and season with salt and pepper. Bring to the boil, reduce the heat and simmer gently for about 20 minutes until the vegetables are tender.

Purée the soup in a liquidizer or food processor until smooth, then return to the saucepan, adjust the seasoning if necessary and when very hot, pour into individual bowls. Garnish with chives.

Serves 4–6
Preparation time 15 minutes
Cooking time: 35 minutes

Spinach & Oatmeal Broth

50 g/2 oz butter

1 onion, chopped

20 g/¾ oz flake oatmeal

275 g/9 oz spinach

50 g/2 oz potatoes, diced

750 ml/1¼ pints chicken stock

pinch grated nutmeg

65 ml/2½ fl oz milk or cream

salt and pepper

For the garnish:

grated nutmeg

flake oatmeal

Melt the butter in a large saucepan and fry the onion until soft but not coloured. Stir in the oatmeal and continue to cook until the oatmeal is beginning to colour slightly.

Wash the spinach, remove any tough stalks and chop the leaves roughly. Add to the pan along with the potatoes, stock and nutmeg and season with salt and pepper. Bring to the boil and then reduce the heat and simmer gently for 10–20 minutes until the spinach is just cooked.

Purée in a liquidizer then return to the pan and add the milk or cream. Taste and adjust the seasoning if necessary. Bring to the boil and serve immediately sprinkled with a little nutmeg and flake oatmeal.

COOK'S NOTES
Use sorrel instead of spinach or a mixture of both. Cook for the minimum time to retain the colour.

Serves 4–6
Preparation time: 5 minutes
Cooking time: 40 minutes

Lentil & Bacon Broth

Rinse the ham shank in cold water then put it into a large saucepan and cover with water. Bring to the boil. This will remove any excess salt from the ham and bring any scum to the surface. Pour off this water, rinse the pan and start again with 2.5 litres/4 pints fresh cold water. Add the lentils, onions, carrots and turnip, bring to the boil, then reduce the heat and simmer for 1½ hours. Add the potatoes and cook for a further 30 minutes until the meat is tender and the broth rich and thick.

Remove the ham from the broth, peel off the skin and cut the meat into small cubes. Return to the broth, season to taste and stir in the parsley.

Serves 8–10
Preparation time: 15 minutes
Cooking time: 2 hours

1 ham shank from 500 g–1 kg/1–2 lb in weight

175 g/6 oz split red lentils, rinsed

2 large onions, finely diced

2 large carrots, finely diced

175 g/6 oz turnip, finely diced

500 g/1 lb potatoes, finely diced

3 tablespoons finely chopped parsley

salt and pepper

Carrot & Herb Soup

Melt the butter in a large saucepan, add the vegetables and garlic and cook gently over a low heat until soft but not coloured. Add the stock, bouquet garni and mace and season with salt and pepper. Bring to the boil then reduce the heat and simmer gently for 45 minutes–1 hour until the vegetables are tender.

Remove the bouquet garni and purée the soup in a liquidizer or food processor until smooth. Return to the saucepan, add the cream and bring to the boil. Mix the herbs together and stir three-quarters of them into the soup. Serve in individual soup bowls garnished with the croûtons and remaining herbs.

COOK'S NOTES
To make croûtons, remove the crusts from 2 slices of bread and cut each slice into 5 mm/¼ inch cubes. Fry in a little hot oil until golden brown on all sides. Drain on absorbent kitchen paper before use.

Serves 6
Preparation time: 10 minutes
Cooking time: 1 hour

25 g/1 oz butter

1 large onion, finely sliced

500 g/1 lb carrots, sliced

1 small potato, sliced

1 clove garlic, chopped

1 litre/1¾ pints chicken stock

1 bouquet garni

pinch ground mace

150 ml/¼ pint cream

2 tablespoons finely chopped coriander

1 tablespoon finely chopped parsley

1 tablespoon finely chopped chervil

salt and pepper

croûtons, see Cook's Notes, to garnish

Mushroom Soup with Crispy Bacon

50 g/2 oz butter

1 onion, finely chopped

1 clove garlic, finely chopped

375 g/12 oz mushrooms, thinly sliced

2 tablespoons plain flour

600 ml/1 pint vegetable or chicken stock

150 ml/¼ pint milk

1 tablespoon Manzanilla sherry (optional)

150 ml/¼ pint single cream

4 rashers bacon, derinded and cooked until crisp and broken into small pieces

salt and pepper

sprigs of fresh chervil, to garnish

Melt the butter in a large pan and fry the onion, garlic and mushrooms until soft and beginning to colour. Sprinkle on the flour and stir to combine. Gradually pour on the stock and milk, stirring well to blend. Bring to the boil, then reduce the heat and simmer for approximately 15–20 minutes.

Add salt and pepper to taste, along with the sherry, if using, and half the cream. Reheat, then divide between 4–6 individual soup bowls. Whip the remaining cream until it is just holding its shape, then spoon a little on top of each bowl of soup. Sprinkle with the bacon pieces and garnish with a sprig of fresh chervil.

COOK'S NOTES
A mixture of cultivated and wild mushrooms gives the soup a very special flavour. For a smoother soup, purée before adding the cream.

Serves 4–6
Preparation time: 15 minutes
Cooking time: 20 minutes

Mussel Soup with Saffron & Garlic

Prepare the mussels, see Cook's Notes. Put 25 g/1 oz of the butter in a very large saucepan, add one third of the onion and leek and cook until soft. Add the mussels, bouquet garni and the white wine. Cover with the saucepan lid and cook on a high heat for 4–5 minutes, stirring the mussels from time to time. When all the mussel shells have opened, drain through a piece of muslin lining a sieve set over a bowl to catch the cooking juices. Remove the mussels from their shells, discarding any which haven't opened. Refrigerate until required.

Gently fry the garlic, carrots and celery in the remaining butter until soft. Add the fish stock and the reserved mussel juices. Add the mussels, reserving 12 to garnish the soup. Bring to the boil and cook gently for 20 minutes. Add the saffron, stir in the cream and blend in a liquidizer or food processor until smooth.

Return to the pan, taste and adjust the seasoning if necessary, stir in the reserved whole mussels and return to the boil. Serve immediately in individual soup bowls garnished with chervil fronds.

COOK'S NOTES

To prepare mussels, wash under cold running water and scrape, removing the 'beard' (the hairy attachment protruding from the mussel) and any barnacles attached to the shells. Discard any mussels that are open or damaged.

A bouquet garni is a bunch of fresh herbs generally consisting of parsley stalks, a sprig of thyme, a bay leaf and a blade of mace tied together. This is added to soups and stews to give additional flavour.

Serves 4–6
Preparation time: 30 minutes
Cooking time: 25 minutes

30–40 fresh, live mussels, approximately 1.5 kg/3 lb

75 g/3 oz butter

1 onion, finely sliced

175 g/6 oz leek, white part only, finely sliced

2 bouquet garni, see Cook's Notes

125 ml/4 fl oz dry white wine

2 cloves garlic, crushed

175 g/6 oz carrot, finely sliced

1 celery stick, finely sliced

750 ml/1¼ pints fish stock, see page 44

pinch saffron

150 ml/¼ pint double cream

salt and pepper

fronds of chervil, to garnish

Game Broth with Potato & Herb Dumplings

1.5 litres/2½ pints game stock, see Cook's Notes

1 onion, finely diced

1 carrot, finely diced

1 celery stick, finely diced

125 g/4 oz turnip, finely diced

1 large potato, finely diced

sprigs of parsley, to garnish

For the dumplings:

15 g/½ oz butter

1 tablespoon finely chopped onion

250 g/8 oz potatoes, cooked and mashed

1 tablespoon semolina

2 tablespoons finely chopped parsley

pinch chopped thyme

pinch nutmeg

beaten egg, to bind

about 2 tablespoons plain flour

salt and pepper

Put the game stock, onion, carrot, celery, turnip and potato into a large saucepan, bring to the boil, then reduce the heat and simmer for 20 minutes until the vegetables are tender.

Meanwhile, prepare the dumplings. Melt the butter in a saucepan and fry the onion until soft but not coloured. Stir the softened onion into the potatoes along with the semolina, parsley, thyme and nutmeg and season with salt and pepper. Add a little beaten egg and enough flour to make a stiff mixture. Roll teaspoons of this dough into 16 balls using a little flour to keep the mixture from sticking. Drop the dumplings into the hot soup and cook gently for 10 minutes until they float. Divide the dumplings between 8 soup bowls and ladle on the broth. Garnish each bowl with a sprig of parsley and serve immediately.

COOK'S TIP
This is an excellent way of using leftover carcasses, bones and trimmings from roast game.

To make the stock, heat a little oil in a pan and brown 750 g/1½ lb carcass, bones etc. with 1 large carrot, 1 onion and 1 leek and 1 celery stick, roughly sliced. Add 1.25 litres/2¼ pints water and a bunch of herbs. Bring to the boil then simmer gently for at least 2 hours before straining.

Serves 8
Preparation time: 20 minutes
Cooking time: 30 minutes

Farmhouse Broth

Put the meat into a large saucepan with 1.8 litres/3 pints water and bring to the boil. Skim the scum from the surface, then add all the remaining ingredients, except the parsley. Reduce the heat and simmer gently for 2–3 hours until the meat is tender and the soup thick.

Lift the meat from the pot, remove from the bone, discard excess fat and cut into thin strips. Return to the soup, taste and adjust the seasoning if necessary and stir in the parsley.

This soup is traditionally eaten with a freshly boiled, floury potato served in the middle; this makes a very substantial snack or main meal.

Serves 8–10
Preparation time: 20–30 minutes
Cooking time: 2–3 hours

375–500 g/12 oz–1 lb shin or brisket of beef on the bone

25 g/1 oz split green peas

25 g/1 oz red lentils

25 g/1 oz pearl barley

125 g/4 oz leek, white and green parts, finely chopped

125 g/4 oz carrot, finely chopped

50 g/2 oz turnip, finely chopped

1 onion, finely chopped

1 celery stick, finely chopped

salt and pepper

2 tablespoons finely chopped parsley, to garnish

Ham & Pea Soup

Melt the butter in a pan and fry the onion, carrot and two-thirds of the bacon gently until soft; this will take about 15 minutes. Add the drained split peas, bay leaf, ham bone and 1.2 litres/2 pints water. Bring to the boil then reduce the heat and simmer gently for 1 hour.

Remove from the heat and discard the ham bone. Season with pepper and salt if necessary. Return the saucepan to the heat. Fry the remaining bacon in a hot pan until crisp, then add to the soup along with 1 tablespoon of the chives. Serve in individual soup bowls and garnish with the remaining chives.

Serves 6
Preparation time: 10 minutes, plus soaking time
Cooking time: 1¼ hours

50 g/2 oz butter

1 large onion, roughly chopped

1 large carrot, roughly chopped

4 thick rashers of bacon, approximately 175 g/6 oz, derinded and diced

250 g/8 oz yellow or green split peas (soaked for 4–6 hours, then drained)

1 small bay leaf

1 ham bone

salt and pepper

2 tablespoons finely chopped chives

starters & snacks

The introduction of a first course, other than soup, is a very recent addition to the traditional Irish menu of soup, main course and pudding. In this section, many of Ireland's best loved products are used to create a tempting overture to the meal. Some of the dishes owe their origins to natural country thrift, where it was considered wrong to waste anything, even the left overs, hence the black puddings and pâtés. Even in 'lean times' some sustenance could be found in the foods gathered from the woods and seashore.

Grilled Goats' Cheese on Soda Bread with Bacon & Tomatoes

1 farl of soda bread, split in half

2 slices cut from a cylindrical goats' cheese, 1 cm/½ inch thick

6 cherry tomatoes, halved

1 tablespoon oil

4 rashers back bacon, cut into strips

4–5 chives, cut in 2.5 cm/ 1 inch lengths

2 sprigs of chervil or dill, to garnish

Using a pastry cutter slightly larger than the diameter of the goats' cheese, cut a circle from each half of the soda farl. Toast the cut side until pale golden in colour. Place a circle of cheese on top and put under a preheated hot grill for 3–4 minutes until the cheese is beginning to melt and turning golden on top. Heat the cherry tomato halves at the same time.

Meanwhile, heat the oil in a pan and fry the bacon strips until crisp and browning. Drain well on absorbent kitchen paper. Place the pieces of toasted bread and cheese in the centre of two serving plates. Arrange the tomatoes and bacon around the toasted cheese and sprinkle with the chives. Garnish with the fresh herb sprigs.

COOK'S NOTES
Irish blue cheese such as Cashel Blue or Rathgore make an excellent alternative to the goats' cheese. For a light snack or lunch serve 2 pieces of the grilled cheese per person with a mixed leaf salad.

Serves 2
Preparation time: 5 minutes
Cooking time: 5–8 minutes

Did you ever eat a forkful

And dip it in the lake

Of heather flavoured butter,

That your mother used to make?

(TRADITIONAL RHYME)

Wild Mushroom Omelette

Melt two-thirds of the butter in a small frying pan and cook the mushrooms until soft but holding their shape. Keep warm.

Put the eggs and 1 teaspoon cold water into a small bowl, season with salt and pepper and add the herbs. Beat lightly with a fork to blend. Stir in the mushrooms.

Melt the remaining butter in a 20 cm/8 inch omelette or non-stick frying pan and when foaming pour on the egg mixture. Quickly stir the egg 3–4 times with a fork, then pull the egg from the edges of the pan into the centre, tilting the pan so that the liquid egg can flow towards the hot surface. When the liquid egg ceases to flow and the omelette looks set but still soft on top, it is cooked.

Using a spatula, fold the edge of the omelette that is closest to the frying pan handle towards the centre and then the opposite edge on top. Turn the omelette out onto a warm plate seam-side down. Garnish with a sprig of parsley and serve immediately.

COOK'S NOTES

The omelette can also be made with cultivated mushrooms or a combination of cultivated and wild mushrooms of whatever varieties are available.

Serves 1

Preparation time: 10 minutes
Cooking time: 5–8 minutes

25 g/1 oz butter

50 g/2 oz wild mushrooms, cleaned, trimmed and sliced

3 eggs

1 teaspoon finely chopped herbs, such as parsley, chives and chervil

salt and pepper

sprig of flat leaf parsley, to garnish

Cockles & Mussels with Bacon

50 fresh, live mussels, approximately 2.75 kg/ 6 lb, washed, scrubbed, barnacles and beard removed, see Cook's Notes, page 19

30 cockles, approximately 375 g/12 oz, washed and scrubbed

8 rashers streaky bacon, derinded

50 g/2 oz butter

1 onion, finely chopped

2 tablespoons finely chopped parsley

1 teaspoon finely chopped chives

salt and pepper

4 sprigs of watercress, to garnish

Put the prepared mussels in a large saucepan. Add 300 ml/½ pint water, bring to the boil, cover and cook quickly for 5 minutes, shaking the pan occasionally during the cooking. Add the cockles and continue cooking for a further 3–5 minutes. When the shells open, the shellfish are cooked. Any unopened shells should be discarded. Remove the cockles and mussels from the shells.

Cut the bacon rashers in half widthways. Roll each piece neatly and secure with a wooden cocktail stick. Put in a pan of boiling water for a few minutes to remove the salt and set the rolls. Drain, dry and discard the cocktail sticks.

Melt the butter in a large frying pan and fry the bacon rolls until coloured. Remove from the pan and keep warm. Fry the onion until soft then add the mussels, cockles and herbs and season with salt and pepper. Toss in the butter to heat thoroughly. Divide evenly between 4 warm serving plates, scatter over the bacon rolls and garnish with a sprig of watercress. Serve with Irish Oatcakes (see page 126) and a glass of Guinness.

COOK'S NOTES
This can be made entirely with either mussels or cockles and served as a main course with boiled potatoes. For a main course serving, double the quantities.

Serves 4
Preparation time: 30 minutes
Cooking time: 8–10 minutes

Fresh Grilled Dublin Bay Prawns with Garlic & Herb Butter

8 whole fresh Dublin Bay prawns in the shell, each weighing no less than 125 g/4 oz

125 g/4 oz butter

1 clove garlic, crushed

4 tablespoons mixed herbs, such as parsley, tarragon and chervil, very finely chopped

salt and pepper

For the garnish:

½ lemon cut into 2 wedges

sprigs of watercress and herbs

Cut the prawns in half lengthwise, remove the gut and wash under cold running water. Dry with absorbent kitchen paper. Lay the prawns shell side down on a baking sheet. Blend the butter, garlic and herbs together and season with pepper and a little salt. Spread over the prawn flesh and cook under a preheated, very hot grill for 3–4 minutes.

Arrange simply on warm plates and garnish with the lemon, sprigs of watercress and herbs. Serve immediately with Irish Wheaten Bread (see page 128).

Serves 2
Preparation time: 5 minutes
Cooking time: 3–4 minutes

Baked Scallops with Garlic & Herbs

Butter 4 scallop shells or similar size ovenproof dishes with half the butter. Combine the breadcrumbs, garlic and herbs and season with pepper. Divide half this mixture evenly between the containers. Arrange the scallops on top and cover with the remaining crumb mixture and the remaining butter cut into small pieces. Set the shells on dishes on a baking sheet and bake in the preheated oven for approximately 10–12 minutes. Be careful not to over-cook the scallops or they will become tough. The wobbly flesh, when cooked, should be only just set. If, when the scallops are cooked, the crumbs aren't golden in colour, quickly put the dishes under a hot grill to finish.

Serve very hot, garnished with lemon wedges and watercress sprigs and accompanied by Irish Wheaten Bread (see page 128).

COOK'S TIP
Scallops can be bought either fresh or frozen. If bought fresh, ask your fishmonger to clean them for you, reserving the shells, which make wonderful containers for many seafood dishes. You will be left with the nut of white meat and the crescent shaped orange/pink roe or coral.

Serves 4
Preparation time: 10 minutes
Cooking time: 10–12 minutes
Oven temperature: 220°C (425°F), Gas Mark 7

125 g/4 oz butter

50 g/2 oz fresh white breadcrumbs

1 clove garlic, finely chopped

1 tablespoon finely chopped parsley

1 tablespoon finely chopped coriander

8 large scallops, shelled, cleaned and both the white and coral sliced in rings

pepper

For the garnish:

1 lemon, cut into 4 wedges

4 sprigs of watercress

Oysters & Guinness

The most popular way of eating oysters has always been in their raw state, fresh from the shell, sometimes with a squeeze of lemon, sometimes with a little cayenne pepper, but always washed down with a glass of creamy Guinness.

6–12 fresh, tightly closed oysters, washed and scrubbed

crushed ice

For serving:

1–2 thick lemon wedges

cayenne pepper (optional)

Irish Wheaten Bread (see page 128)

butter, for the bread

glass of Guinness

Open the oysters just before serving by holding each one firmly in a thick cloth. Insert a strong sharp knife, an old fashioned pointed can opener or a screwdriver into the hinge of the shell. Give a sharp twist upwards and prize off the shell. If you have difficulty opening the oysters from the hinge, try to prize the shells open by inserting the knife at the side of the shell. Take care not to lose the oyster juices.

Loosen the oyster, leaving it in the deep half of the shell which has retained the juices. Arrange these on a bed of crushed ice on a large serving plate. Serve with lemon wedges, a dusting of cayenne pepper, if desired, wheaten bread and butter and a glass of creamy Guinness.

Cook's Notes

Oysters should only be eaten like this when bought fresh and alive from a good fishmonger. The shells should be tightly closed and can be stored for several days if carefully packed in ice and well refrigerated.

Serves 1–2
Preparation time: 5 minutes

The secret will never be known,

She cannot discover,

The breath of her lover,

But thinks it as sweet as her own.

(JONATHAN SWIFT)

Irish Smoked Salmon with Potato Cakes, Sour Cream & Chives

250 g/8 oz potatoes, boiled and mashed

pinch salt

25 g/1 oz butter, melted

50 g/2 oz plain flour, plus extra for shaping and cooking

snipped chives, to garnish

For serving:

250–300 g/8–10 oz smoked salmon, thinly sliced

2 tomatoes, seeds removed and diced

4 tablespoons thick soured cream

First prepare the potato cakes. Put all the ingredients into a bowl and mix gently with a wooden spoon to form a light dough. Turn onto a lightly floured surface and roll into a circle about 1 cm/ ½ inch thick. Cut into 4 circles using a 5 cm/2½ inch plain cutter.

Warm a heavy frying pan over a gentle heat until a light dusting of flour just begins to turn a very pale fawn colour. Keep the pan at this temperature and add the potato cakes. Cook for a few minutes until lightly browned on each side.

While the potato cakes are cooking, divide the salmon between 4 serving plates, arranging it on one side. Allow the potato cakes to cool slightly then place one on each plate beside the salmon. Arrange the tomato on top of each potato cake, top with soured cream and garnish with chives. Serve immediately.

COOK'S NOTES
You can double quantities of the ingredients given for the potato cakes and use the extra potato cakes for serving with bacon and eggs as part of an Ulster Fry (see page 58). They are also good eaten hot with butter and home-made jam.

Serves 4
Preparation time: 10 minutes
Cooking time: 8 minutes

Irish Smoked Salmon with Wheaten Bread

I believe that there is only one way to eat the best smoked salmon and that is cut in generous slices with the finest wheaten bread – naturally both from Ireland.

Arrange the smoked salmon slices on 4 serving plates. Serve with buttered wheaten bread and garnish with a lemon wedge.

Freshly ground black pepper, finely chopped onion and capers are the traditional garnish but I think, with such a fine product, the delicate taste of the fish should not be overpowered by additions.

COOK'S NOTES

Smoked salmon can be bought ready sliced in pre-prepared packs; in whole sides, sliced or unsliced; or cut to order from delicatessens and fishmongers. When pre-sliced it is generally cut thinly, when cutting it yourself, more generous slices can be allowed. Good quality smoked salmon should be moist and delicate in colour.

You can make a quick smoked salmon pâté by mixing equal quantities of smoked salmon pieces or trimmings and curd or soft cheese in a food processor with lemon juice and black pepper. Allow 50 g/2 oz salmon and 50 g/2 oz cheese per portion.

Serves 4
Preparation time: 5 minutes

250–300 g/8–10 oz Irish smoked salmon, sliced

Irish Wheaten Bread (see page 128)

butter, for the bread

1 lemon, quartered into wedges

Irish Smoked Salmon with Scrambled Eggs

15 g/½ oz butter

3 large eggs

1 tablespoon milk

1 tablespoon cream
(optional)

25–40 g/1–1½ oz smoked
salmon, cut into narrow
strips

1 teaspoon finely snipped
chives

1–2 slices warm wheaten
bread, toasted and buttered

salt and pepper

Melt the butter in a saucepan until foaming. Place the eggs in a bowl and mix well with a fork. Add the milk and season with salt and pepper. Pour the eggs into the foaming butter. Stir with a wooden spoon, over a gentle heat, scraping the bottom of the pan and bringing the outside edges to the middle. The scrambled eggs are cooked when they form soft creamy curds and are barely set. Remove from the heat, stir in the cream, if using, salmon and chives and pile onto the hot brown toast on a warm serving plate. Serve immediately.

COOK'S NOTES
Salmon slices, trimmings or off-cuts are excellent for this dish and dill makes an interesting alternative to the chives.

Serves 1
Preparation time: 5 minutes
Cooking time: 3–4 minutes

fish & seafood

Ireland's crystal clear rivers and streams, and the seas which surround the island have always been a rich source of food for the people. Whether it be salmon, king of fish, or the humble herring, the noble oyster or the simple cockle, there has always been an abundant supply to be had for the fishing or the taking. These would have been simply poached to retain the best of their character, flavour and appearance, or added to a pie or tart to feed a large family.

Cod & Prawn Bake in Cheese Sauce

450 ml/¾ pint milk

quarter of an onion

6 peppercorns

blade of mace

bay leaf

a few parsley stalks

50 g/2 oz butter

450 g/1 lb cod fillets, skin and bones removed

50 g/2 oz button mushrooms, sliced

125 g/4 oz cooked peeled prawns

30 g/1½ oz plain flour

1 tablespoon lemon juice

125 g/4 oz grated Cheddar cheese

salt and pepper

Put the milk into a saucepan with the onion, peppercorns, blade of mace, bay leaf and parsley stalks. Bring to the boil, then remove from the heat and leave to infuse while preparing the remaining ingredients.

Melt the butter in another saucepan and use a little to brush the inside of a 1.6 litre/2¾ pint ovenproof pie dish. Cut the cod into finger-size strips, place in the pie dish and scatter the mushrooms and prawns on top. Strain the milk through a sieve, then discard the contents of the sieve. Add the flour to the remaining butter in the saucepan, stirring to blend. Gradually stir in the strained milk to make a smooth sauce. Bring to the boil, stirring continually until the sauce thickens. Season with salt, pepper and lemon juice and add two-thirds of the grated cheese. Stir until melted. Pour the sauce over the fish, sprinkle with the remaining cheese, place on a baking sheet and cook in the preheated oven for 20–25 minutes until golden brown. Serve with Irish Wheaten Bread (see page 128) and salad.

COOK'S NOTES
Any firm fleshed fish or shellfish can be used for this dish along with cultivated or wild mushrooms. The bake can also be made in 4 individual pie dishes each holding approximately 300 ml/ ½ pint or in 8 scallop shells which makes an excellent starter.

Serves 4
Preparation time: 15 minutes
Cooking time: 20–25 minutes
Cooking temperature: 180°C (350°F), Gas Mark 4

Creamy Salmon Kedgeree

50 g/2 oz butter

1 large onion, finely chopped

175 g/6 oz long grain rice, cooked until just tender

500 g/1 lb cooked salmon, bones removed and broken into large flakes

3 hard boiled eggs, roughly chopped

2 tablespoons finely chopped parsley

150 ml/¼ pint single cream

salt and pepper

1 teaspoon finely chopped chives, to garnish

Melt half the butter in a large pan and fry the onion until soft. Stir in the rice and season well with salt and pepper. Add the salmon, eggs, parsley and cream, folding them carefully into the rice to prevent the fish and eggs from breaking up too much. Pile into an ovenproof dish, cover with buttered foil and heat thoroughly in the preheated oven for 15 minutes. When hot, serve sprinkled with the chives.

COOK'S NOTES
Any white fish or smoked fish such as haddock or smoked salmon can also be used to make the kedgeree. A combination of fresh and smoked salmon is particularly good.

The single cream can be omitted but it helps to keep the dish moist.

A curry sauce is sometimes added for moisture and additional flavour.

Serves 4
Preparation time: 15 minutes
Cooking time: 15 minutes
Oven temperature: 180°C (350°F), Gas Mark 4

Baked Trout with Herb Stuffing & Cream Sauce

Melt 50 g/2 oz of the butter in a large frying pan and fry the onion until soft but not coloured. Remove from the heat. Mix the herbs together and add half to the pan along with the breadcrumbs, lemon rind, juice and nutmeg and season with salt and pepper. Mix well and moisten with 1–2 tablespoons of the cream. Divide this mixture equally between the 4 fish, using it to stuff the belly of each.

Butter a large ovenproof baking dish with half the remaining butter. Lay the stuffed trout head to tail in the baking dish, dot with the remaining butter and pour over the wine, if using. Bake in the preheated oven for 20 minutes until slightly firm to the touch. Pour the cooking liquor into a saucepan and boil rapidly, reducing by half. Add the remaining cream and herbs and return to the boil adjusting the seasoning if necessary.

Arrange the fish on individual warm serving plates, pour a little sauce over each fish and serve with boiled potatoes and crisp green vegetables or salad.

COOK'S NOTES
Brown trout are a wild freshwater fish, native to Ireland and found in the rivers, lakes and streams throughout the country. They are a fine delicate fish with a slightly nutty flavour.

Serves 4
Preparation time: 20 minutes
Cooking time: 20 minutes
Cooking temperature: 240°C (475°F), Gas Mark 9

75 g/3 oz butter

1 small onion, finely chopped

2 tablespoons finely chopped parsley

1 tablespoon finely chopped chives

3 teaspoons finely chopped dill

50 g/2 oz fine white breadcrumbs

finely grated rind of ½ lemon

2 teaspoons lemon juice

pinch nutmeg

250 ml/8 fl oz single cream

4 rainbow or brown trout, approximately 300– 325g/ 10–11 oz each, cleaned

150 ml/¼ pint dry white wine (optional)

salt and pepper

Fried Trout with Toasted Hazelnuts & Herbs

4 trout, approximately 300–325 g/10–11 oz each, gutted, washed and dried, heads and tails left on

125 g/4 oz plain flour

250 g/8 oz butter (125 g/ 4 oz clarified), see Cook's Notes

125 g/4 oz hazelnuts, shelled

2 tablespoons lemon juice

2 tablespoons finely chopped parsley

1 tablespoon finely chopped chives

salt and pepper

For the garnish:

1 lemon, cut into 4 wedges

watercress sprigs

Season the fish well, inside and out and toss in the flour shaking off the excess. Fry in the clarified butter (see Cook's Notes) until golden brown, about 5 minutes on each side, carefully turning once only to prevent the skin from breaking.

While the trout are cooking, toast the hazelnuts under the grill until the skins can be easily rubbed off, then chop roughly. Quickly melt the remaining butter in a small pan, allow it to foam and turn brown, then add the lemon juice. Transfer the cooked trout to 4 warm serving plates. Scatter the nuts on top of each trout and keep warm. Pour the browned butter on top of the fish. Scatter over the herbs and garnish with lemon wedges and watercress. Serve with boiled new potatoes and a green vegetable or a salad.

COOK'S NOTES

To clarify butter: put the butter in a small saucepan, bring to the boil and let it bubble several times without browning. Remove from the heat, allow to settle then carefully pour through a sieve lined with damp muslin. This will catch all the salty sediment which causes butter to burn.

Serves 4
Preparation time: 10–15 minutes
Cooking time: 6–8 minutes

Grilled Salmon Steaks with Herb Butter

Mix the butter, herbs and lemon juice in a bowl. Lay the butter on a piece of greaseproof paper and roll into a log shape about 2.5 cm/1 inch in diameter. Refrigerate until solid.

Wash and dry the salmon steaks. Brush a baking sheet with melted butter and lay the steaks on top. Brush with half of the remaining butter and season well with salt and pepper. Cook under a preheated medium grill for about 4–5 minutes on each side. On turning each steak, brush with more melted butter and season again. Alternatively, the steaks can be cooked on a cast-iron grill pan.

Cut the log of herb butter into four circles. Transfer the cooked steaks carefully on to warm plates and top each with a circle of butter. Garnish with lemon wedges and sprigs of watercress and serve with boiled new potatoes, steamed vegetables or a green salad.

COOK'S NOTES

For ease of eating, the skin and central bones of the steaks can be removed before serving but this needs to be done with care otherwise the fish can loose its shape. It is best done on the serving plate, the skin and bones being removed before the fish is garnished and served.

Serves 4
Preparation time: 15 minutes
Cooking time: 8–10 minutes

125 g/4 oz butter

2 tablespoons mixed herbs such as parsley, dill, chervil, chives or fennel, very finely chopped

squeeze of lemon juice

4 salmon steaks about 175–250 g/6–8 oz each (2–2.5 cm/¾–1 inch thick)

50 g/2 oz butter, melted

salt and pepper

For the garnish:

4 lemon wedges

sprigs of watercress

Roast Fillet of Salmon with Saffron Cream Sauce

4 salmon fillets, about
150–175 g/5–6 oz each

oil, for frying and roasting

salt and pepper

1–2 tablespoons finely
snipped chives, to garnish

For the sauce:

150 ml/¼ pint fish stock,
see Cook's Notes

150 ml/¼ pint dry white
wine

4 strands saffron

150 ml/5 fl oz single
cream

Season the salmon with salt and pepper. Heat a little
oil in a large frying pan until hot and place the salmon in the pan
flesh side down. Cook for about 2 minutes over a high heat to
brown. Transfer the salmon to a lightly oiled baking sheet, skin
side down, season and finish cooking in the preheated oven for
about 7–9 minutes, depending on the thickness of the fillet. The
flesh should be opaque pink when cooked.

While the fish is roasting make the sauce by combining the
stock, wine and saffron in a saucepan. Bring to the boil, reduce
the heat and simmer until reduced by half. Add the cream, bring
to the boil and boil continuously until the sauce thickens and
coats the back of a spoon.

Serve the fish in the centre of a large plate with the sauce
poured around and garnished with chives. Accompany with
steamed seasonal vegetables and boiled new potatoes.

COOK'S NOTES
*Fish Stock: for 1.2 litres/2 pints stock, sweat 250 g/8 oz chopped
white vegetables in butter until soft, add 500 g/1 lb washed white
fish bones and trimmings. Pour on 150 ml/¼ pint dry white wine,
1 litre/1¾ pints water and the juice of 1 lemon. Simmer for
20 minutes and strain before use.*

Serves 2
Preparation time: 2–5 minutes
Cooking time: 9–11 minutes
Oven temperature: 240°C (475°F), Gas Mark 9

Salmon Fish Cakes

Combine the potatoes, flaked fish, Tabasco sauce or cayenne pepper, if using, lemon juice and parsley in a large bowl and season well with salt and pepper; mix well to combine. Bind with the egg yolk. Turn the mixture onto a lightly floured surface and form into a thick roll about 28 cm/11 inches long and 5 cm/ 2 inches thick. Cut into 8 even-sized pieces and shape each into neat cakes approximately 75 g/3 oz in weight, 6 cm/2½ inches in diameter and 2 cm/¾ inch thick.

Dip the cakes in the beaten egg and coat evenly with breadcrumbs. Place the oil and butter in a frying pan and fry the fish cakes for approximately 5 minutes on each side until they are crisp, golden and very hot. Drain well on absorbent kitchen paper and serve with fresh tomato sauce and lemon wedges.

COOK'S NOTES

Fish cakes in Ireland were traditionally made with salmon because it was free for the catching. Today, however, salmon being more expensive, it can be substituted by any white fish such as cod, haddock or whiting. A combination of smoked and fresh fish is also good.

Serves 4
Preparation time: 20 minutes
Cooking time: 10 minutes

250 g/8 oz cooked, mashed potatoes

500 g/1 lb salmon, cooked, skinned and flaked

few drops Tabasco sauce or ½ teaspoon cayenne pepper (optional)

1–2 tablespoons lemon juice

2 tablespoons finely chopped parsley

1 large egg yolk, beaten

plain flour, for dusting

1 large egg, size 2, beaten

125–175 g/4–6 oz fresh white breadcrumbs

1 tablespoon oil

50 g/2 oz butter

salt and pepper

For serving:

fresh tomato sauce

4 lemon wedges

Steamed Mussels in White Wine Sauce

50 g/2 oz butter

1 large onion, finely chopped

1–2 cloves garlic, finely chopped

1 small leek, white and green parts, finely sliced

2 kg/4 lb live mussels, prepared, see Cook's Notes page 19

300 ml/½ pint dry white wine

25 g/1 oz plain flour

2 tablespoons finely chopped parsley

1-2 tablespoons double cream (optional)

salt and pepper

Melt half the butter in a very large saucepan and gently fry the onion, garlic and leek until soft but not coloured. Add the mussels, white wine and 150 ml/¼ pint water, cover and bring to the boil. Cook for 2–5 minutes until the mussels open, shaking the pan several times during the cooking. Using a draining spoon, divide the mussels between 4 large soup plates, discarding any that haven't opened during cooking. Keep warm.

Mix the remaining butter with the flour to form a paste and little by little add to the juices in the pan, stirring to thicken. Bring to the boil, season to taste, stir in the parsley and pour over the mussels. Serve immediately with wheaten or soda bread. Just before serving, 1–2 tablespoons double cream can be added to the sauce for extra richness, if you like.

COOK'S NOTES
Allow about 500 g/1 lb mussels per person, the equivalent of 600 ml/1 pint, about 15–20 mussels if you are fortunate enough to be able to gather them yourself. For cooking I use a preserving pan, shaking and turning the mussels continually, bringing those nearest the heat to the top of the pile to ensure that they all cook quickly and evenly.

Serves 4
Preparation time: 15 minutes
Cooking time: 8 minutes

God be with the happy times,

When the troubles we had not,

And our mothers made colcannon,

In the three-legged pot. (TRADITIONAL RHYME)

Dressed Crab

Traditionally, crabs and other shellfish were gathered by the locals from the many bays along the coast. Eaten in greater quantity, they were once the main source of protein for coastal dwellers. Today they are enjoyed as an affordable luxury, most often eaten as Dressed Crab and served with salad.

1 live crab, approximately 875 g/1¾ lb

2–3 tablespoons fine white breadcrumbs

¼–½ teaspoon English mustard

salt and pepper

squeeze of lemon juice

For the garnish:

1 hard boiled egg, white chopped, yolk sieved

1–2 tablespoons finely chopped parsley

sprigs of watercress

lemon wedges

Plunge the crab into a large pan of boiling salted water. Cover and simmer for 25 minutes. Remove from the water and leave to cool.

Lay the crab on its back and twist off the legs and claws. Remove the bony tail flap and discard. Lever off the central body, pulling it free from the shell. This consists of bone with some white crab meat and the 'dead men's fingers'. Discard the 'fingers', the stomach sac from behind the mouth and the mouth itself. Cut the body in half and, using a skewer, pick out the white meat from the crevices. Put into a bowl. Scoop out the soft yellowish brown meat from inside the shell and place in a second bowl. Crack the claws and legs, extract the meat and combine with the reserved white meat. Cream the brown meat, add the breadcrumbs, mustard and season with salt and pepper. Arrange down the centre of the washed and dried shell. Season the white meat with salt, pepper and lemon juice and pile on either side of the brown meat. Garnish with the egg, parsley, watercress and lemon and serve with mayonnaise, wheaten bread and salad.

COOK'S NOTES
It is always best to cook your own crab, that way they not only have a better flavour but you know they are fresh. If only cooked crabs are available, buy them from a reputable fishmonger.

Small heavy crabs will have plenty of meat. To use the shell as a container, enlarge the opening by breaking away the shell along the line of weakness that runs around the shell's rim.

Serves 1
Preparation time: 30 minutes
Cooking time: 25 minutes

Cold Boiled Lobster with Herb Mayonnaise

Remove the claws from the lobster, crack and reserve. Extend the lobster's tail, shell side down and cut in half through its length. Discard the stomach sac in the head, the feathery gills and the dark intestinal vein running down the centre of the tail. Rub the greyish-green liver and the pink roe through a sieve into a mixing bowl, add the remaining ingredients, stirring to combine.

Remove the flesh from the tail shells and cut into slanting slices. Put into a bowl and add enough of the mayonnaise mixture to moisten. Return the lobster meat to the shell halves. Add a little extra mayonnaise for appearance.

Arrange a half lobster on each plate, garnish with a cracked claw, lemon wedge and watercress. Serve with a mixed leaf salad, the remaining herb mayonnaise and buttered wheaten bread.

COOK'S NOTES
When buying any cooked shellfish it is important that they are very fresh. If possible, cook them yourself from live. To cook a lobster, plunge it head first into fast boiling, well salted water, hold down with tongs and boil for 1 ½ minutes, then reduce the heat and simmer for 8–10 minutes per 500 g/1 lb to cook the flesh.

Serves 2
Preparation time: 15–20 minutes

1 cooked lobster, approximately 1 kg/2 lb

1 hard boiled egg, sieved

2 tablespoons finely chopped parsley

2 tablespoons finely chopped chervil

1 teaspoon finely chopped chives

1 tablespoon finely chopped capers

150 ml/¼ pint thick mayonnaise

lemon juice, to taste

For the garnish:

2 lemon wedges

sprigs of watercress

Dublin Lawyer

At one time, lobster, along with other forms of shellfish, were a popular food with those who could catch them. Today they are much less readily available, and this, coupled with increasing demand from restaurants, has made them a luxury item commanding premium prices.

1 live lobster, approximately 1 kg/2 lb

50 g/2 oz butter

1 small onion, finely chopped

4 tablespoons Irish whiskey

150 ml/¼ pint double cream

1 teaspoon English mustard

1 teaspoon lemon juice

salt and pepper

For the garnish:

sprigs of watercress

lemon wedges

Plunge the lobster, head first, into fast boiling salted water for 2 minutes. Remove and hold under cold running water to stop the cooking. Set the lobster on a chopping board board shell side down,extend the lobster's tail and cut lengthwise through the centre dividing it in two. Discard the stomach sac in the head, the feathery gills and the dark intestinal vein running down the centre of the tail. Remove the meat from the shells and cut into chunks. Crack the claws and remove the meat.

Heat the butter in a large frying pan and fry the onion until soft. Add the lobster meat and fry until just cooked, then add the coral and liver. Warm the whiskey, pour over and carefully ignite with a lighted taper. When the flames have died down add the rest of the ingredients and mix well. Put the lobster meat in the warm shells. Boil the liquid to reduce and thicken, pour over the lobster and serve immediately garnished with watercress and lemon wedges.

Serves 2
Preparation time: 20–30 minutes
Cooking time: 20 minutes

Grilled Mackerel with Gooseberry & Fennel Sauce

Season the mackerel inside and out and stuff with the fennel sprigs and stalks, if using. Cut 2–3 diagonal slits on each side of the backbone so that the heat can penetrate more quickly. Brush both the fish and a baking sheet lightly with oil and set the prepared fish on top.

Prepare the sauce by combining the gooseberries with 125 ml/4 fl oz water in a large saucepan. Bring to the boil then add the sugar, butter and fennel. Cook gently for 6–7 minutes until the berries burst but still have texture.

While the sauce is cooking, place the mackerel under a preheated grill and cook for 4–7 minutes on each side, depending on the size, turning very carefully. Remove the herb stuffing and serve immediately, garnished with lemon wedges and sprigs of fennel. Accompany with the hot gooseberry sauce and boiled new potatoes.

COOK'S NOTES
Mackerel, being a very oily fish, needs a sharp sauce to offset the richness of the flesh. Gooseberries or other sharp fruit such as rhubarb are traditional but sorrel and mustard are also popular.

Herrings can also be cooked in this way.

Serves 4
Preparation time: 5–10 minutes
Cooking time: 8–15 minutes

4 small mackerel, approximately 275 g/9 oz each, gutted, washed and dried

fresh fennel sprigs, fronds and stalks (optional)

oil, for brushing

For the sauce:

375 g/12 oz gooseberries, topped and tailed

2 tablespoons sugar

25 g/1 oz butter

1 tablespoon finely chopped fennel

salt and pepper

For the garnish:

4 lemon wedges

4 sprigs of fennel

Herb Stuffed Herrings with Mustard Sauce

4 herrings, approximately
125 g/4 oz each, prepared,
see Cook's Notes

For the stuffing:

75 g/3 oz butter

1 small onion, finely
chopped

2 tablespoons parsley,
finely chopped

1 teaspoon dill, finely
chopped

2 hard boiled eggs, finely
chopped

grated rind of ½ lemon

50 g/2 oz breadcrumbs

salt and pepper

For the sauce:

25 g/1 oz butter

25 g/1 oz plain flour

300 ml/½ pint milk

1 tablespoon lemon juice

1 tablespoon prepared
English mustard

1 tablespoon finely
chopped parsley

For the garnish:

4 lemon wedges

4 sprigs of flat leaf parsley

To make the stuffing, melt half the butter in a saucepan and fry the onion until soft. Use the rest of the butter to grease an ovenproof dish and a sheet of foil. Add the remaining stuffing ingredients to the onion and season well to taste. Divide the stuffing between the 4 fish, re-shaping them carefully, to make sure the stuffing doesn't fall out. Lay each herring carefully in the dish, cover with the buttered foil and bake in the preheated oven for 40–45 minutes.

While the fish is baking, prepare the sauce by melting the butter, stirring in the flour and gradually adding the milk to form a smooth paste. Cook gently for about 5 minutes, stirring all the time, until the sauce is thick and the flour cooked. Stir in the lemon juice, mustard and parsley and season to taste.

Serve the herrings with lemon wedges, flat leaf parsley, the hot mustard sauce and boiled new potatoes.

COOK'S NOTES

To prepare a herring, scrape off the scales from tail to head. Cut off the fins and gut slitting the belly from behind the head to the vent, pull out the viscera. Run the point of a knife down the backbone to release any blood and wash under cold running water, dry well.

Serves 4–8

Preparation time: 15–20 minutes
Cooking time: 40–45 minutes
Oven temperature: 160°C (325°F), Gas Mark 3

Fried Herrings in Mustard & Oatmeal

Spread a little mustard inside each herring. Coat in the beaten egg and roll each one in the seasoned oatmeal, pressing it evenly over the fish.

Heat the fat or oil in a large frying pan and cook the herrings gently for about 4 minutes on each side until an even golden brown colour. Drain on absorbent kitchen paper, garnish with lemon wedges and watercress and serve with boiled new potatoes.

COOK'S NOTES

If the herrings are small allow 2 per person. Although it is traditional to serve the herrings with the heads on, they can be removed before cooking. The backbone can also be removed and the herring flattened before being coated and fried. This way, fry the flesh side first.

Herrings can be bought ready prepared from the supermarket, delicatessen or fishmonger. When scraping the scales from the fish, work from the tail end to the head. Cut off the fins with a pair of kitchen scissors. The herrings can be prepared more simply by omitting the egg, mustard and oatmeal and just dipping in flour before frying.

Serves 4
Preparation time: 15 minutes
Cooking time: 8–10 minutes

4 herrings, approximately 125 g/4 oz each, gutted, scaled, fins removed, washed and dried

1–2 tablespoons prepared English mustard

1 egg, beaten

75 g/3 oz oatmeal, seasoned with salt and pepper

bacon fat or oil, for frying

salt and pepper

For the garnish:

1 lemon, cut in wedges

sprigs of watercress

Smoked Fish Pie

A favourite in many Irish homes on a Friday, where the tradition of not eating meat on this day is still practised. Fish pie can simply be made with plain white fish or a combination of smoked and white fish.

500 g/1 lb smoked haddock

450 ml/¾ pint milk

50 g/2 oz butter

1 onion, finely chopped

175 g/6 oz mushrooms, sliced

25 g/1 oz plain flour

1 teaspoon prepared English mustard

2 tablespoons finely chopped parsley

1 tablespoon lemon juice

2–3 eggs, hard boiled and roughly chopped

salt and pepper

For the topping:

875 g/1¾ lb potatoes, cooked and mashed

25 g/1 oz butter, melted

3–4 tablespoons milk

50 g/2 oz Cheddar cheese, grated

Put the haddock in a shallow saucepan, pour on the milk, heat slowly until simmering and cook for 5–10 minutes.

Meanwhile, melt the butter in a pan and fry the onion until soft but not coloured. Add the mushrooms and continue to fry until colouring. Stir in the flour and cook gently for about 1 minute, then remove from the heat.

When the fish is cooked, strain the liquor into a jug and gradually add to the onion and mushroom mixture, stirring well. Bring to the boil and simmer for 10 minutes until thick, stirring continually. Add the mustard, parsley, lemon juice and eggs and season with salt and pepper. Flake the fish, remove the bones and add to the sauce. Pile into a deep ovenproof pie dish.

Mix the potatoes with the melted butter and milk, season well and pile roughly on top of the fish mixture, covering it evenly. Scatter over the cheese and bake in the preheated oven for about 30 minutes until piping hot and crisp.

COOK'S NOTES
When using smoked fish in either this or any other recipe, buy naturally smoked, undyed fish. The best quality smoked haddock is Finnan Haddie. For extra flavour add 6 peppercorns, a blade of mace, 1 bay leaf, 1 wedge of onion and 2 cloves to the milk, while cooking the fish.

Serves 4–6
Preparation time: 20–30 minutes
Cooking time: 35–40 minutes
Oven temperature: 190°C (375°F), Gas Mark 5

meat

Although cattle were originally bred mainly for their milk, and sheep for their wool, their meat was highly prized by the country's kings and noblemen and was served at formal banquets and feasts. Its' importance was such that the rank and status of the guests was determined by the cuts of roast meat that they were offered. Today, beef and lamb are still important elements of the meal in most households. Pork and bacon have always been less expensive and therefore more accessible.

An Ulster Fry

This is one of Ireland's most famous dishes. It differs from a Scottish or English 'fry' in that it is served with a selection of fried Irish breads: potato bread, soda bread and dropped scones. It also commonly includes fried black and white puddings.

oil, for frying

1–2 sausages

2 bacon rashers, back and streaky, derinded

2 slices black or white pudding

½ Soda Farl (see page 124)

1 Potato Bread, halved (see page 129)

1 Drop Scone (see page 137)

1 tomato, halved

1–2 eggs, size 2

sprigs of watercress, to garnish

Heat a little oil and fry the sausages until almost cooked, then add the bacon rashers and black or white pudding and continue to fry. Remove from the pan and drain on a plate lined with absorbent kitchen paper. Keep warm. Fry the soda bread and potato bread until lightly toasted, drain and keep warm. Fry the tomato halves, skin side down, until softened but still holding their shape, then remove and keep warm. Add a little extra oil to the pan, heat and fry the egg or eggs, spooning the hot fat on top of the yolk and white until cooked to your liking. Arrange all the fried ingredients on a hot plate, garnish with the sprigs of watercress and serve immediately.

COOK'S NOTES
An Ulster Fry can be served at any time of the day, for breakfast, lunch, high tea or supper, not to mention as a snack. Mushrooms, onions, liver, chops and fried potatoes can also be added if a more substantial meal is required!

Serves 1

Pork Ribs & Onions

1 kg/2 lb pork spare ribs

500 ml/1 pint water or stock

2 large onions, sliced

1 bay leaf, parsley stalks, 1 stick of celery and 1 blade of mace tied together

1 tablespoon cornflour

2 tablespoons finely chopped parsley

salt and pepper

Wash the ribs and cut into manageable sized portions. Put into a large saucepan and add the water or stock. Bring to the boil and skim. Add the onions, herbs and season with salt and pepper. Cover, reduce the heat and simmer for 2–2½ hours until the pork is tender and beginning to fall from the bone. Blend the cornflour with a little of the cooking liquid, then return to the pan to thicken. Add the parsley, taste and adjust the seasoning if necessary and serve with boiled potatoes and a glass of Guinness.

Serves 4
Preparation time: 5 minutes
Cooking time: 2–2½ hours

Roast Stuffed Pork Fillet

50 g/2 oz butter

1 large onion, finely chopped

175 g/6 oz fresh white breadcrumbs

grated rind of ½ lemon

pinch dried thyme

1 ½ tablespoons finely chopped parsley

a little beaten egg to bind

2 pork fillets of even size, approximately 375 g/12 oz each

salt and pepper

For the gravy:

1 tablespoon arrowroot

300 ml/½ pint stock

Melt half the butter in a pan and fry the onion until soft but not coloured. Stir in the breadcrumbs, lemon rind, herbs and season to taste. Use a little beaten egg to bind. Leave to go cold.

Slit the pork fillets lengthways without cutting right through them and flatten the meat until the fillets lie flat. Arrange the stuffing on top of one of the fillets turning in the tails at both ends. Lay the second fillet on top also tucking in the ends and wrapping the long sides around to encase the stuffing. Tie at intervals with string. Heat the remaining butter in an ovenproof dish and brown the fillets. Pour on 150 ml/¼ pint water, cover tightly and cook in the preheated oven for 1–1¼ hours. Remove the string and transfer to a warm serving dish. Thicken the cooking juices with the arrowroot blended in the stock, then taste and adjust the seasoning if necessary. Serve the fillet carved in slices and accompanied by apple sauce.

Serves 4
Preparation time: 30 minutes
Cooking time: 1–1¼ hours
Oven temperature: 180°C (350°F), Gas Mark 4

Lamb's Liver with Bacon & Onions

Place a little oil in a pan and fry the bacon until brown and beginning to crisp. Remove from the pan and keep warm. Fry the onion in the fat remaining in the pan until soft and just beginning to colour. Remove from the pan and keep warm with the bacon. Place the flour in a large polythene bag and season with salt and pepper. Add the slices of liver, one at a time, to coat evenly in the flour, shaking off any excess. Add a little extra oil to the pan and quickly fry the liver until brown on both sides and cooked through. Divide the liver, bacon and onions between 2 serving plates and serve immediately with Champ (see page 101).

Serves 2
Preparation time: 10 minutes
Cooking time: 10–15 minutes

a little oil, for frying

4 rashers bacon, derinded

1 large onion, sliced

2 tablespoons plain flour

500 g/1 lb lamb's liver, sliced

salt and pepper

Pressed Ox Tongue

Put the tongue in a pan, cover with water and bring to the boil. Drain and rinse, return to the pan and cover with water. Add the onion stuck with cloves, peppercorns, carrot, celery and herbs. Bring to the boil and simmer for 4 hours. Cool slightly in the liquid; strain and reserve the liquid. Remove the tongue and plunge into cold water. Remove the skin, root and small bones. Curl the tongue to fit into a tongue press or straight sided dish.

Mix the gelatine in a heatproof bowl with a little cold water, then set in a saucepan of hot water. Stir and melt until clear, then add to the reserved liquid. Pour over the tongue, cover and weigh down to press. Leave in the refrigerator overnight to set before turning out. Slice thinly to serve.

Serves 6
Preparation time: 10–15 minutes
Cooking time: 4–5 hours, plus soaking overnight and pressing

1 salted ox tongue 1.5–2.75 kg/3–6 lb, soaked in cold water overnight

1 large onion, stuck with 5 cloves

6–8 peppercorns

1 large carrot, halved

2 celery sticks, halved

2 bay leaves

a few parsley stalks and a sprig of thyme

2 teaspoons powdered gelatine

Baked Irish Ham

Until recent years, pork and bacon were central to the diet of the Irish. As a result, there are a wide variety of traditional recipes for the various cuts of pork. The sides of the pig were known as the 'flitch' and cured as bacon, whilst the hind legs were cured as ham.

2 kg/4 lb joint of bacon or ham, cooked and rind removed (see Boiled Bacon and Cabbage, right)

4 tablespoons demerara sugar

whole cloves

150 ml/¼ pint ham stock

Set the cooked joint in a roasting tin. Mark a diamond pattern over the fat with a knife at 2.5–3.5 cm/1–1½ inch intervals. Press the demerara sugar into the fat, completely covering the top and sides. Stick a clove in the centre of each diamond. Pour the stock into the roasting dish around the joint. Cook in the preheated oven for 20 minutes until the fat is crisp and brown. Serve carved in slices (you will get 10–12) with roast potatoes or Champ (see page 101), boiled cabbage wedges, braised red cabbage, cauliflower, carrots, celery or leeks.

COOK'S NOTES
If the joint of bacon or ham is being baked from cold, use a lower oven temperature, 180°C (350°F), Gas Mark 4, and cook for 30–45 minutes.

Serves 6–8
Preparation time: 5–10 minutes
Cooking time: 20 minutes
Oven temperature: 220°C (425°F), Gas Mark 7

Boiled Bacon & Cabbage

Drain the bacon, then put into a large saucepan, cover with fresh cold water and bring to the boil. Discard the water, rinse the bacon, wash out the pan and begin again with fresh water, adding all the ingredients except the cabbage. Bring to the boil, cover the pan and simmer for 25 minutes per 500 g/1 lb.

Add the cabbage wedges 20–25 minutes before the end of the cooking time and continue to cook until the bacon and cabbage are tender. Remove the bacon and cabbage from the cooking liquid and drain the cabbage well. Peel the rind from the bacon and serve in slices with the cabbage wedges, boiled potatoes and parsley sauce.

COOK'S NOTES
A 2 kg/4 lb joint of bacon when cooked will give approximately 10–20 slices, depending on whether the meat is carved hot or cold, plus a 150 g/5 oz tail piece, which makes an ideal pie filling.

Serves 6–8
Preparation time: 10–15 minutes, plus soaking overnight
Cooking time: 1 hour 40 minutes

. . and the kale and praties blended

Like the pictures in a dream. (Traditional Rhyme)

2 kg/4 lb joint of bacon, smoked or unsmoked, tied in a neat shape and soaked overnight in cold water

1 onion, quartered

2 carrots, quartered

2 celery, sticks, quartered

1 leek, quartered

2 bay leaves, sprig thyme, parsley stalks and blade of mace tied together

10 peppercorns

1 tight headed green Irish cabbage, cut into wedges, core removed, for serving

Irish Spiced Beef

2–2.75 kg/4–6 lb beef, topside or silverside

selection of flavourings, such as onions, parsnips, turnips, carrots, celery and a bunch of herbs

300 ml/½ pint Guinness (optional)

For the pickle:

5 teaspoons ground bay leaves

2 teaspoons ground cloves

3 teaspoons ground ginger

3 teaspoons ground mace

1 teaspoon pepper

½ teaspoon ground allspice

4 cloves garlic, crushed

6 tablespoons brown sugar

250 g/8 oz spiced pickling mixture or 25 g/1 oz saltpetre and 500 g/1 lb coarse salt

3.35–3.95 litres/6–7 pints cold water

Tie the meat into a neat shape. Combine all the spicing ingredients in a large glass bowl, mix well and add the meat. Make sure there is enough liquid to cover. Cover and refrigerate for 1 week, turning daily.

When pickled, put into a large pot with the flavourings. Cover with water, bring to the boil and simmer for 2–2½ hours. During the last 30 minutes of cooking the Guinness can be added for extra flavour, if liked.

When cooked, remove the meat from the cooking liquor, wrap tightly in greaseproof paper and foil to set the shape and leave to go cold. Refrigerate overnight before serving carved in slices with pickles.

COOK'S NOTES

Boned and rolled brisket of beef, also known in Ireland as top breast of beef, can be used. It cuts into very neat circular slices, but takes 4–5 hours to cook.

Traditionally saltpetre was used for spicing beef, but, it is not always easy to obtain nowadays. Spiced pickling mixture however, which should have the saltpetre already added, can be obtained from your butcher.

Serves 6–12
Preparation time: begin preparations 1 week before serving
Cooking time: 2–2½ hours

Beef & Guinness Stew

Season the flour with salt and pepper and toss the meat in the flour. Heat the oil in a large saucepan or casserole and fry the beef cubes until browned all over. Add the onion and cook for a few minutes then stir in any remaining flour. Add the carrot, Guinness and 750 ml/1¼ pints water, stirring well to combine. Bring to the boil, add the bay leaf, cover and simmer gently for 1½–2 hours until the meat is tender. Alternatively cook in a preheated oven for the same length of time.

Half an hour before the end of the cooking time, add the prunes. Remove the bay leaf, taste and adjust the seasoning if necessary, sprinkle with the parsley and serve with baked potatoes in their jackets.

COOK'S NOTES
Thick plate and shin of beef can also be used for this stew, the shin meat being removed from the bone before cooking. The bone can be tucked down the side of the stew during the cooking then removed before serving. This gives additional flavour. Individual slices of meat can also be cooked in this way and are equally delicious.

Serves 4
Preparation time: 20–30 minutes
Cooking time: 1½–2 hours
Oven temperature, if using: 150–160°C (300–325°F),
Gas Mark 2—3

50 g/2 oz plain flour

1 kg/2 lb top side of beef, cut in 2.5cm/1 inch cubes

oil, for frying

1 large onion, peeled and sliced

1 large carrot, peeled and thickly sliced

300 ml/½ pint Guinness

1 bay leaf

125 g/4 oz pitted prunes, soaked in water

salt and pepper

2 tablespoons finely chopped parsley

Fillet Steak with Cashel Blue Cheese & Croûtons

50 g/2 oz Cashel Blue cheese

1 fillet steak approximately 200–250 g/ 7–8 oz cut 3.5–4.5 cm/ 1½–1¾ inches thick

25 g/1 oz butter

5 g/¼ oz croûtons (see page 17)

few sprigs of thyme

sprigs of watercress, to garnish

salt and pepper

Trim the rind from the cheese and slice it until you have enough to cover the top of the fillet steak. Season the fillet with salt and pepper and seal on both sides in a little butter on a very hot pan. Transfer to a buttered baking sheet and set the cheese on top. Put into a very hot oven for 5 minutes for rare; 8 for medium rare and 15 minutes for well done, allowing the cheese to melt and lightly colour. Transfer the steak from the baking sheet to a hot plate, scatter round the croûtons and a few sprigs of thyme and pour around the cooking juices. Garnish with sprigs of watercress. Serve immediately.

COOK'S NOTES
Cashel Blue is one of Ireland's most famous cheeses and, in addition to being an important element on the cheese board, has many uses in the kitchen. It is perfect in soup, as a topping for toasted bread, scones and pies and it can also be used in stuffings for fillet of beef and breast of chicken.

Serves 1
Preparation time: 5 minutes
Cooking time: 5–15 minutes
Oven temperature: 220°C (425°F), Gas Mark 7

Beef Steak & Oyster Pudding

750 g/1 ½ lb topside beef

50 g/2 oz plain flour, seasoned with salt and pepper

oil, for frying

1 large onion, finely chopped

125 g/4 oz mushrooms, sliced

150 ml/¼ pint beef stock

150 ml/¼ pint Irish dry stout

1 bay leaf

1–2 tablespoons chopped parsley

12 fresh oysters and their juice

For the pastry:

50 g/8 oz plain flour

15 g/½ oz baking powder

125 g/4 oz shredded suet

25 g/1 oz butter

salt

Trim the beef and cut into 25 cm/1 inch cubes. Toss the meat in the seasoned flour and fry until browned. Transfer to a saucepan. Heat the oil and fry the onion until soft. Then add the mushrooms and continue to fry until lightly browned. Add the meat with the stock, stout, bay leaf and parsley. Bring to the boil, then simmer for 1–1½ hours, Leave the steak pudding filling to go cold, then stir in the oysters and their juice. Chill.

Sieve the flour, baking powder and salt into a bowl, mix in the suet, then stir in 150 ml/¼ pint water to make a firm dough. Don't over mix or overwork the pastry. Roll out to a circle about 32.5 cm/13 inches in diameter. Mark the circle into 4 and cut out one triangular wedge. Roll this out for the lid to a circle about 18 cm/7 inches in diameter.

Lightly butter a 1 litre/2 pint pudding basin and line with the suet pastry to stand 2 cm/1 inch above the bowl. Fill with the steak and oyster mixture. Set the pastry lid on top, brush the rim with water and fold over the upstanding pastry pressing to seal together. Cover with a piece of buttered foil and steam in a steamer or pan half-filled with hot water for 1½-1¾ hours, topping up with boiling water as required.

COOK'S NOTES

50 g/2 oz fresh suet, chopped, and 50 g/2 oz dried shredded suet can be used as an alternative to all dried suet. The pastry will benefit from resting and chilling for 30 minutes before using.

If there is too much sauce with the filling reserve the excess, heat up and serve as extra gravy with the pudding.

Serves 4–6
Preparation time: 30 minutes
Cooking time: 1½–2 hours

Ulster Steak

Toss the meat in the seasoned flour. Heat the oil in a large frying pan and brown well on all sides. Transfer to a flameproof casserole. Fry the mushrooms for a few minutes to colour slightly and add to the meat with the onions, the rest of the flour and other ingredients. Bring to the boil, cover and simmer for 1½–2 hours until the meat is tender. Add a little extra water if the liquid reduces too much – the sauce should be quite liquid and should be 'mopped' up with mashed potatoes, champ or fresh soda bread.

COOK'S NOTES
Seasoned flour is flour to which salt and pepper to flavour has been added.

Sometimes sliced carrots are added to this recipe and stout is used instead of water or stock – both are delicious and so quick to prepare.

Serves 4–5
Preparation time: 15–20 minutes
Cooking time: 1½–2 hours

750 g–1 kg/1½–2 lb topside, cut into individual portions 2 cm/¾ inch thick

50 g/2 oz flour, seasoned with salt and pepper

oil, for frying

175 g/6 oz button mushrooms

1 large onion, sliced

2 teaspoons mushroom ketchup

1 tablespoon brown sauce

900 ml/1½ pints water or beef stock

salt and pepper

Gaelic Steak

Heat the butter and oil in a frying pan and fry the onion until soft but not coloured. Scrape to the side of the pan, increase the heat and fry the steak on both sides until cooked as required. Remove the meat from the pan and keep warm. Add the whiskey to the pan and set alight; when the flames have subsided pour on the cream and mix with the onion and meat juices. Bring to the boil, adjust the seasoning, add the parsley and pour over the meat. Serve immediately garnished with sprigs of watercress.

COOK'S NOTES
A thin slice of well hung rump steak can also be used instead of the fillet or sirloin steak. This takes a much shorter time to cook. It is necessary to flame the whiskey to burn off the alcohol, and concentrate the flavour. A more pleasant tasting sauce will result.

Serves 1
Preparation time: 10 minutes
Cooking time: 5–20 minutes

15 g/½ oz butter

1 tablespoon oil

3 tablespoons onion, finely chopped

1 x 250-300 g/8–10 oz fillet or sirloin steak, trimmed of excess fat

1 measure (about 25 ml/ 0.83 fl oz) Irish whiskey

6–8 tablespoons double cream

1 tablespoon finely chopped parsley

sprigs of watercress, to garnish

salt and pepper

Minced Beef in Pastry

Beef dishes combined with pastry, such as Steak and Kidney Pie, Minced Beef Tart and Beef Wellington have been popular in Ireland for many years, as has the versatile Meat Loaf. This family recipe combines elements from them all and is quick and easy to prepare.

500 g/1 lb minced beef

1 small onion, grated

1 clove garlic, crushed

1 small carrot, grated

50 g/2 oz white breadcrumbs

1 tablespoon tomato purée

1 tablespoon Worcestershire sauce

1 tablespoon finely chopped parsley

pinch mixed herbs

salt and pepper

For the pastry:

500 g/1 lb frozen puff pastry

flour, for rolling

1 egg, beaten

Combine all the ingredients for the filling, then press into a log shape approximately 7 x 25 cm/3 x 10 inches. Leave to chill in the refrigerator. Roll the pastry thinly to a 30 cm/12 inch square and cut off a 5 cm/2 inch strip for decoration. Set the log of meat along the long end of the pastry, brush the edges with a little beaten egg and fold over the remaining pastry to form a neat package. Press the edges to seal well and finish with a shell pattern or the prongs of a fork. Cut decorations for the top from the pastry strip. Stick these on with beaten egg. Set the pastry log on a baking sheet, brush with beaten egg and bake in the preheated oven for 45 minutes until golden brown. Serve hot or cold, cut in slices, with a rich tomato sauce, see Cook's Notes page 72.

COOK'S NOTES
Four individual parcels can be made in the same way but on a smaller scale. In both cases, the onion and carrot needs to be finely grated, as it is uncooked before baking.

Serves 4
Preparation time: 30 minutes
Cooking time: 45 minutes
Oven temperature: 220°C (425°F), Gas Mark 7

Boiled Silverside with Dumplings

Heat a little oil in a large saucepan then brown the meat. Add the cloved onion, bunch of herbs, 600 ml/1 pint water and the stout. Bring to the boil then simmer for 2 hours until the meat is tender. Three quarters of the way through the cooking time, remove the cloved onion and herbs and add the whole vegetables.

Meanwhile, make the dumplings. Sift the flour into a bowl, stir in the suet, parsley and salt and pepper, then mix to a dough with the egg and water. About 15 minutes before the end of the cooking time, roll into small balls and drop into the simmering liquid.

Serve the meat on a hot dish surrounded by the vegetables and dumplings. Accompany by boiled potatoes and some of the cooking liquor in a sauceboat.

COOK'S NOTE
If boned and rolled brisket, or top breast as it is sometimes called, is used, it takes 4–5 hours to cook but is also delicious.

Serves 6
Preparation time: 30 minutes
Cooking time: 2–2½ hours
Oven temperature: 220°C (425°F), Gas Mark 7

oil, for frying

1.75–2 kg/3½–4 lb silverside of beef, tied into a neat shape

1 onion, stuck with 6 cloves

parsley, bay leaf and celery stick, tied together

300 ml/½ pint stout

12–16 small pickling onions, peeled

500 g/1 lb small carrots,

For the dumplings:

125 g/4 oz self-raising flour

50 g/2 oz shredded suet

2 tablespoons finely chopped parsley

1 egg (size 2), beaten with 4 tablespoons cold water

salt and pepper

Irish Meat Loaf

50 g/2 oz butter

25 g/1 oz browned breadcrumbs, see Cook's Notes below

1 small onion, finely chopped

500 g/1 lb minced beef

125 g/4 oz white breadcrumbs

1 tablespoon tomato ketchup

1 teaspoon Worcesteshire sauce

1 teaspoon crushed juniper berries

1 tablespoon finely chopped chives

1 tablespoon finely chopped parsley

1 teaspoon finely chopped oregano

1 egg, beaten

salt and pepper

Grease a 19 x 9 x 5.5 cm/7½ x 3¾ x 2¼ inch loaf tin with half the butter and dust with the browned breadcrumbs. Heat the remaining butter in a saucepan and fry the onion until soft, then add the beef and continue to cook until browning. Stir in the remaining ingredients and pack tightly into the prepared tin. Cover with foil and bake in the preheated oven for 1–1½ hours until firm to the touch. Leave to rest for 10–15 minutes before turning out. Serve cut in slices either hot or cold. A rich tomato sauce is a tasty accompaniment, see Cook's Notes.

COOK'S NOTES

To make browned breadcrumbs, toast fresh white breadcrumbs in the oven until dry and golden brown.

This meat loaf mixture can also be used to make meat balls. Cook them in this delicious spicy tomato sauce made from 1 chopped onion and 1 chopped garlic clove, fried until soft, then add 1 x 425 g/14 oz can plum tomatoes, 65 ml/2½ fl oz stock and a pinch each of sugar, basil, cinnamon and salt and pepper, then simmer for 20 minutes.

Serves 4
Preparation time: 15–20 minutes
Cooking time: 1–1¼ hours
Oven temperature: 190°C (375°F), Gas Mark 5

Oxtail Stew

Oxtail, although once widely used in the preparation of soups and stews, is less frequently used today. However, this particular stew is rich and delicious and well worth remembering.

Heat the oil in a pan and fry the oxtail until well browned, then transfer to an ovenproof casserole dish. Fry the onion, also until brown, and add to the oxtail with the flour and tomato purée. Pour on the liquid and stir to blend. Add the carrots, thyme, bay leaf, mace and season with salt and pepper. Bring to the boil. Cover, reduce the heat and simmer very gently for 3–3½ hours until the meat is tender and falling off the bone. The stew can also be cooked in a preheated oven for the same length of time. Skim off excess fat, taste and adjust the seasoning, if necessary, and serve with mashed potatoes, champ or jacket potatoes. Steamed celery hearts and broccoli are excellent accompaniments.

COOK'S NOTES
Oxtail stew is inclined to be quite fatty. For the best results make the day before, refrigerate overnight and just before use remove the fat which will have solidified on top.

Serves 4–6
Preparation time: 20–30 minutes
Cooking time: 3–3½ hours
Oven temperature, if using: 150–160°C (300–325°F), Gas Mark 2–3

1 large oxtail, about 1.5 kg/3 lb, cut into 5 cm/ 2 inch lengths

oil, for frying

1 large onion, sliced

50 g/2 oz plain flour

2 tablespoons tomato purée

1.5 litres/2½ pints beef stock, water, Guinness or red wine

2 large carrots, sliced

1 sprig of thyme

1 bay leaf

pinch powdered mace

salt and pepper

But lest your kissing should be spoiled,

Your onions must be thoroughly boiled.

(Jonathan Swift)

Irish Stew

One of Ireland's most famous dishes, traditionally made with mutton, but nowadays, since mutton is rarely available, lamb chops from the neck or shoulder, or stewing lamb, baked off the bone, is used instead.

1 kg/2 lb neck of lamb, cut into rings about 1.5 cm/ ¾ inch thick

2 large onions, sliced

1 kg/2 lb 'floury' potatoes, sliced

2 large carrots, sliced

2–3 tablespoons finely chopped parsley

400 ml/14 fl oz lamb stock or water

salt and pepper

Layer the meat and vegetables in a deep saucepan or flameproof casserole dish. Sprinkle over half the parsley and season between each layer with salt and pepper; finish with a layer of potatoes. Pour over the stock or water and cover tightly with a piece of buttered greaseproof paper. Cover this with foil and a tightly fitting lid. Bring to the boil, then reduce the heat and simmer very gently for 1½–2 hours either on the hob or in the preheated oven until the meat is tender, the liquid well absorbed and the stew rich and pulpy. If the potatoes are waxy in texture they will not break down into the liquid. To thicken the juices, remove a few of these slices, mash them and return to the pan. Add the remaining parsley, taste and adjust the seasoning, if necessary, and serve with a glass of stout.

COOK'S NOTES
Broad shoulder chops or stewing lamb removed from the bone can also be used for Irish Stew. The carrots are not traditional but they make a more tasty and interesting dish.

The cooking liquid could be half stock and half Guinness as an alternative, this is also not traditional!

Serves 4
Preparation time: 20 minutes
Cooking time: 1½–2½ hours
Oven temperature, if using: 160°C (325°F), Gas Mark 3

poultry &
game

Poultry has always been an important food and source of income, even for the poorest families. A hen could be bought, bartered or stolen and, once acquired, cost practically nothing to keep. The eggs could not only be eaten, but exchanged for other groceries when money was short. Today, 'white' meat has become more desirable for the health conscious and poultry has never been more popular. Game however, is still the choice for the more sophisticated palate and the rural huntsman and his family.

Pigeon, Steak and Mushroom Pie

50 g/2 oz plain flour

6 pigeon breasts, approximately 750 g/1½ lb, cut into 2.5 cm/1 inch cubes

750 g/1½ lb chuck steak, cut into 2.5 cm/1 inch cubes

oil, for frying

1 large onion, finely chopped

300 g/10 oz mushrooms, sliced

200 ml/7 fl oz Guinness

200 ml/7 fl oz beef or game stock

1 bay leaf and parsley stalks

½ teaspoon allspice powder

1 tablespoon chopped parsley

salt and pepper

For the pastry:

500 g/1 lb flaky or puff pastry

flour, for rolling

1 egg, size 4, beaten

Season the flour with salt and pepper and toss the pigeon and the steak in the flour. Fry in batches, in the hot oil, until brown. Transfer to a large casserole and add any remaining flour. Fry the onion and mushrooms until lightly browned and add to the meat. Pour on the Guinness and boil scraping up any residue stuck to the pan. Add to the casserole with the remaining ingredients and season with salt and pepper. Bring to the boil, cover and simmer for about 1½ hours until the meat is tender. Leave to go cold.

Remove the bay leaf and parsley stalks and put into a 1.2 litre/2 pint pie dish with a pie funnel. Roll out the pastry on a floured surface and cover the pigeon and steak mixture, making a double crust around the pie dish rim, sealing well and fluting the edges. Decorate with the pastry trimmings, brush with beaten egg and bake in the preheated oven for 20–25 minutes until risen and golden brown. Serve hot.

COOK'S NOTES
Alternatively, the casserole can have a crumble topping. Rub 50 g/2 oz butter into 175 g/6 oz plain flour, add 1 tablespoon mixed fresh herbs and 50 g/2 oz grated hard cheese. Spread over the stew and bake in a preheated oven at 180°C (350°F), Gas Mark 4 for 20–25 minutes.

Serves 4–6
Preparation time: 45 minutes
Cooking time: about 2 hours, plus cooling time
Oven temperature: 220°C (425°F), Gas Mark 7

Boned Stuffed Chicken

125 g/4 oz butter

1 large onion, finely chopped

250 g/8 oz fine white breadcrumbs

1 tablespoon finely chopped parsley

1 tablespoon finely chopped chervil

1 tablespoon finely chopped tarragon

1 egg, beaten

1 x 2–2.5 kg/4–5 lb roasting chicken, boned, with the skin unpunctured

2 large slices frying ham, cut 2.5 mm/⅛ inch thick, rind removed

375 g/12 oz pork sausage meat

300 ml/½ pint hot chicken stock

salt and pepper

Melt half the butter in a pan and fry the onion until soft but not coloured. Stir in the breadcrumbs, herbs and season with salt and pepper. Bind with the beaten egg. Leave to go cold. To bone the chicken, see Cook's Notes.

Stuff the chicken. Pull the wings and legs through to the inside and flatten the flesh of the bird. Lay the two slices of ham over the breast meat, divide the sausage meat in half and spread over the ham. Lay a log of the stuffing down the centre from top to tail. Fold over the sides of the chicken tucking in excess flesh and skin at the neck and tail. Don't stretch otherwise the skin will burst. Stitch the edges together.

Set in a roasting pan, breast side up. Rub with the remaining butter, pour on the stock and cook in the preheated oven for approximately 2 hours. Serve hot or cold, cut into about 20 slices.

COOK'S NOTES

To bone the chicken, cut off the ends of the legs and wings at the first joints and remove the wishbone. Place the bird breast side down on a board and cut along the backbone, working from the tail to the neck end. Scrape away the flesh from the rib cage, working down one side of the bird until the wing is reached. Ease the knife between the ball and socket joint and sever from the rib cage, while keeping it attached to the skin. Continue easing away the flesh from the bone until you reach the leg joint. Sever the ball and socket joint. Continue in this way until you reach the breastbone. Turn the chicken and repeat the process on the other side of the bird. Separate the breastbone from the skin. Finally, lay the chicken flat on a board with the skin side down. Scrape the flesh away from the wing bone and remove. Repeat the process with the other wing bone and with both the leg bones.

Serves approximately 12–15
Preparation time: 30–40 minutes, plus boning the chicken
Cooking time: about 2 hours
Oven temperature: 190°C (375°F), Gas Mark 5

Traditional Pot Roast Chicken with Parsley Stuffing

Melt the butter in a pan and fry the onion until soft. Stir in the breadcrumbs, chopped herbs and season with salt and pepper. Bind with the beaten egg. Leave to go cold.

Heat the oil in a pan and fry the bacon and button onions until brown. Transfer to a large pot or ovenproof casserole. Stuff the chicken breast and body cavity. To truss the chicken, see Cook's Notes.

Brown the trussed bird all over in the remaining fat. Set on top of the onions and bacon, and add the remaining ingredients. Bring to the boil, cover and simmer until cooked. Transfer the chicken to a large serving dish, surround with the vegetables and keep warm while making the sauce.

Blend a tablespoon of butter and flour together and gradually whisk into the boiling cooking liquid until it thickens. Season to taste, strain and serve with the chicken.

COOK'S NOTES

Trussing keeps the stuffing in position and also holds the bird together so that it will sit easily for carving. To truss a bird, set it breast up and pull back the legs. Push a threaded trussing needle through the bird at the joint of one knee. Turn the bird on to its breast, pull the neck skin over the neck cavity and secure with a stitch which passes through both the wings. Next, turn the bird on to its side, pull the ends of the string from both the neck and the wing together and fasten them firmly. Finally, turn the bird breast side up, tuck the tail into the body cavity and tie the drumsticks together by stitching, in a figure of eight, under the breast bone and around the drumsticks.

Serves 4–6
Preparation time: 30 minutes, plus trussing
Cooking time: 1¼–1½ hours
Oven temperature: 180°C (350°F), Gas Mark 4

50 g/2 oz butter, plus extra for thickening the sauce

1 large onion, finely chopped

125–150 g/4–5 oz fine white breadcrumbs

3 tablespoons finely chopped parsley

pinch dried mixed herbs

1 small egg, beaten

2 tablespoons oil

250 g/8 oz bacon, in a piece, rind removed and cut into large cubes

12 button onions, peeled

1 x 1.75–2.25 kg/3½–4½ lb roasting chicken, wiped

500 g/1 lb carrots, cut in chunks

250 g/8 oz turnip, cut in chunks

1 bouquet garni

450 ml/¾ pint strong chicken stock

flour, for thickening the sauce

salt and pepper

Chicken Frigasse

750 g/1½ lb cooked boneless chicken breast, cut in large finger strips

175 g/6 oz button mushrooms, fried

16 pickling onions, skinned and boiled

For the sauce:

50 g/2 oz butter

50 g/2 oz plain flour

300 ml/½ pint chicken stock

300ml/½ pint milk

1 egg yolk

65 ml/2½ fl oz double cream

1–2 tablespoons Worcestershire sauce

1 tablespoon mustard

1 teaspoon anchovy sauce

2 teaspoons capers

2 tablespoons finely chopped parsley

salt and pepper

For the garnish:

8 rashers bacon, cut in half, rolled and grilled

4 lemon wedges

bunch of watercress

paprika

Make the sauce, melt the butter in a saucepan, stir in the flour and gradually add the stock and milk until blended. Bring to the boil, stirring continuously until thickened and smooth and cook for a few minutes. Mix the egg yolk and the cream together and whisk into the sauce with the remaining ingredients. Fold in the chicken pieces, stir in the mushrooms and onions and heat thoroughly. Serve on a large flat dish garnished with the bacon rolls, lemon wedges, watercress and a dusting of paprika.

COOK'S NOTES

Frigasse or fricassee is a word used to describe a method of preparing poultry, lamb, veal, rabbit, fish and vegetables by boiling or stewing in stock or milk. This liquid is then thickened with egg yolk and cream and the meat or vegetables served in it.

Serves 4–6
Preparation time: 30 minutes
Cooking time: 15–30 minutes

Rabbit Frigasse

A rich stew of rabbit meat which was a particularly popular dish in large country houses in Ireland, during the eighteenth and nineteenth centuries.

Joint the rabbit, see Cook's Notes.

Cover the rabbit with water and a little salt and vinegar. Soak overnight to whiten and tenderize the flesh. Discard the soaking water, cover with fresh water and bring to the boil. Discard this boiling water then simmer the rabbit in the stock, milk, onions and herbs for 1–2 hours until tender. Reserve the cooking liquor.

Melt the butter in a pan, stir in the flour and gradually add 600 ml/1 pint of the cooking liquor. Bring to the boil, stirring continuously, reduce the heat and simmer until smooth and thick. Stir in the cream and mustard and season with salt and pepper. Add the rabbit pieces along with the fried mushrooms. Heat thoroughly, then serve garnished with the parsley.

COOK'S NOTES
Rabbit bred for the table will take much less time to cook than wild rabbit.

To joint the rabbit, remove the ribs, shoulder and neck, cutting from the body just below the ribs. Use to make stock. Divide the saddle and legs just above the top of the legs, remove the membrane and flap, cut the saddle and the legs in half.

Serves 4
Preparation time: 30 minutes, plus soaking the rabbit overnight
Cooking time: 1–2 hours

1–2 rabbits, to give approximately 1.75 kg/ 3½ lb when prepared

salt

vinegar

600 ml/1 pint chicken stock

300 ml/½ pint milk

2 large onions, thinly sliced

bay leaf, sprig of thyme and parsley stalks tied together

For the sauce:

50 g/2 oz butter

50 g/2 oz plain flour

150 ml/¼ pint cream

1 teaspoon mustard

salt and pepper

For the garnish:

175 g/6 oz button mushrooms, fried in butter

2 tablespoons finely chopped parsley

Venison Stew with Parsnip and Potato Champ

1–2 tablespoons oil

1 onion, finely chopped

750 g–1 kg/1½–2 lb lean venison, off the bone, cut into 2.5 cm/1 inch cubes

25 g/1 oz plain flour

300 ml/½ pint Guinness

750 ml/1¼ pints game stock or water

1 bay leaf

1 sprig marjoram

12–18 pickling onions, peeled

125–175 g/4–6 oz celery, cut in 2.5 cm/1 inch lengths

2 tablespoons finely chopped parsley

salt and pepper

Heat half the oil in a large frying pan and fry the onion until soft and beginning to brown. Transfer to a large flameproof casserole. Heat the remaining oil in a pan and fry the meat, a little at a time, until brown. Mix with the onions. Stir in the flour and add the Guinness and stock along with the bay leaf and marjoram and season with salt and pepper. Bring to the boil then reduce the heat and simmer gently for 1–1½ hours until the meat is almost tender. The stew can also be cooked in the oven for the same length of time. Add the pickling onions and celery 15–30 minutes before the end of the cooking time. Taste and adjust the seasoning if necessary, stir in the parsley and serve with parsnip champ, see Cook's Notes.

COOK'S NOTES
Allow 500 g/1 lb potatoes and 500 g/1 lb parsnips, washed and peeled, for 4 servings. Boil both separately until tender, drain and dry well, then mash together with plenty of butter and salt and pepper.

Serves 4–6
Preparation time: 15 minutes
Cooking time: 1½–2 hours
Oven temperature, if using: 150–160°C (300–325°F), Gas Mark 2–3

Roast Heather Honey Duck with Walnut Stuffing

1 x 2.5–2.75 kg/5–6 lb dressed duckling

2 tablespoons lemon juice

2 tablespoons clear heather honey

2 tablespoons plain flour

300 ml/½ pint duck or chicken stock

salt and pepper

For the stuffing:

1 tablespoon oil or rendered duck fat

1 onion, finely chopped

125 g/4 oz walnuts, chopped

125 g/4 oz fresh white breadcrumbs

grated rind of 1 lemon

1 tablespoon chopped parsley

1 teaspoon marjoram, chopped

1 egg, beaten

Make the stuffing. Heat the oil in a pan and fry the onion until soft. Stir in the walnuts, breadcrumbs, lemon rind, parsley and marjoram and season with salt and pepper. Bind with the egg.

Prick the duck all over with a fine skewer. Fill the body cavity with the stuffing. Truss the duck, see page 81, and set on a wire rack in a roasting tin. Mix the lemon juice and honey together and brush over the duck. Season with salt and pepper. Cook in the preheated oven for 10 minutes, then reduce the heat and cook for 25 minutes per 500 g/1 lb, allowing 10–15 minutes resting time. Baste frequently during the cooking, brushing with any remaining lemon and honey mixture. Remove from the oven and drain off all but 1 tablespoon fat. Stir in the flour blending with the cooking juices, add the stock and boil to thicken for the gravy.

Serve with Roasted Root Vegetables (see page 98) and boiled cabbage (see page 63).

COOK'S NOTES

When roasting any type of meat or poultry, it is important to allow 10–15 minutes resting time before carving to let the flesh relax. Carving straight from the oven can result in tough meat. Cover the meat and keep in a warm place while resting.

Serves 4

Preparation time: 20 minutes
Cooking time: 2–2½ hours
Oven temperature: 220°C (425°F), Gas Mark 7 for 10 minutes, then reduce the temperature to 190°C (375°F), Gas Mark 5 for the remainder of the cooking time.

Roast Goose with Apple and Whiskey Stuffing

1 x 5.5 kg/12 lb goose, oven ready with giblets to make stock

1 Cox's apple, peeled, cored and grated to give approximately 150 g/5 oz

2 tablespoons malt whiskey

25 g/1 oz butter

1 onion, finely chopped

250 g/8 oz coarse white breadcrumbs

2 tablespoons finely chopped parsley

1 tablespoon finely chopped sage

pinch grated lemon rind

1 egg, size 4, beaten

salt and pepper

To truss the goose, see page 81. Prick the bird all over with a fine skewer and set on a wire rack in a roasting tin. Season with salt and pepper. Cook in the preheated oven for 20–25 minutes per 500 g/1 lb. Pour off the fat several times during the cooking. Reserve for future use.

Soak the grated apple in the whiskey. Melt the butter in a pan and fry the onion until soft, then add the soaked apple, breadcrumbs, herbs, lemon rind and season with salt and pepper. Bind with the egg. Grease a 900 ml/1½ pint ovenproof soufflé dish with goose fat and fill with the stuffing. Cover with foil and cook with the goose for 45 minutes. Some of the stuffing can be used to fill the cavity of small Cox's apples which can be baked for 30 minutes with the goose. Rest the goose for 15–20 minutes in a warm place before carving. Serve the goose with gravy, roast potatoes and braised red cabbage.

COOK'S NOTES

In Ireland goose is traditionally served at Michaelmas (29 September) and Christmas when it is said to bring prosperity for the coming year.

The reserved goose fat is excellent for roasting potatoes and parsnips and for greasing baking tins. It will keep in the refrigerator for several months. Use the goose giblets to make stock for the gravy.

Serves 6

Preparation time: 30 minutes
Cooking time: 4–5 hours
Oven temperature: 240°C (475°F), Gas Mark 9 for 30 minutes, then reduce the heat to 190°C (375°F), Gas Mark 5 for 3½–4½ hours.

Roast Pheasant

Use the pheasant giblets to make stock for the gravy. Melt half the butter in a pan, fry the giblets along with the onion, celery and carrot until browned. Pour on the red wine and boil fiercely to reduce by half. Add 450 ml/¾ pint water, the bay leaf and peppercorns, then simmer while preparing and roasting the pheasant.

Smear the pheasant with the remaining butter, season with salt and pepper, set in a roasting dish and cook in the preheated oven for 20–25 minutes per 500 g/1 lb. Baste several times during the cooking. Once the bird is cooked, cover loosely and rest for 10 minutes before carving.

Meanwhile, strain the stock and boil quickly to reduce to 200 ml/7 fl oz. Drain all but 1 tablespoon of fat from the roasting dish, add the flour and stir well to mix with the sediment. Blend in the stock. Boil, strain and keep warm.

Serve the pheasant garnished with watercress and accompanied by brussels sprouts, Roasted Root Vegetables (see page 98), roast potatoes, game chips and gravy.

COOK'S NOTES

Since pheasant is a lean meat with a fine skin it is important to smear it well with butter or oil to protect if from drying out during the cooking and to baste it several times while roasting. It can also be covered with rashers of fatty bacon.

Serves 2

Preparation time: 20 minutes
Cooking time: 35–45 minutes
Cooking temperature: 220°C (425°F), Gas Mark 7

50 g/2 oz butter

pheasant giblets (heart, gizzard and neck), washed

1 small onion, peeled and quartered

1 celery stick, chopped

1 small carrot, sliced

65 ml/2½ fl oz red wine

1 bay leaf

6 peppercorns

1 plump oven ready pheasant, approximately 875 g/1¾ lb, in weight

2 tablespoons plain flour

salt and pepper

watercress, to garnish

Breast of Pheasant with Savoy Cabbage and Mustard Sauce

4–6 tablespoons clarified butter, see Cook's Notes, page 42

4 x 95–150 g/3¾–5 oz pheasant breasts, skin and wing bones removed

salt and pepper

fresh herbs, to garnish

For the sauce:

300 ml/½ pint game stock

300 ml/½ pint red wine

2 tablespoons port

2–4 tablespoons Irish wholegrain mustard

300 ml/½ pint single cream

For serving:

425 g/14 oz Savoy cabbage, shredded

50 g/2 oz butter

Heat the butter in a large frying pan and cook the pheasant breasts skin side down over a gentle heat for 3–4 minutes. Turn and cook on the second side for a further 3–4 minutes. Remove from the heat, season with salt and pepper and leave to rest for 3 minutes before serving.

Make the sauce by combining the stock, wine and port in a saucepan and reducing by half. Stir in the mustard and cream and reduce until the sauce thickens and coats the back of a spoon. Season to taste with salt and pepper.

Cook the cabbage, drain, toss in the butter and season. Divide between the 4 plates, piling it in the centre. Carve each pheasant breast into 3 flat slices and arrange in a fan on top of the cabbage. Spoon a little sauce over each breast and garnish with a fresh herb sprig. Serve with Champ (see page 101).

COOK'S NOTES
Cooking times will vary depending on the depth of the pheasant breast. When cooked the flesh should feel firm but springy to the touch and when sliced should only just be cooked through.

Serves 4
Preparation time: 10 minutes
Cooking time: 6–8 minutes

The farmer's goose, who in the stubble,

Has fed without restraint or trouble,

Grown fat with corn and sitting still,

Can scarce get o'er the barn door sill.

(JONATHAN SWIFT)

vegetable
dishes

Although vegetables, both wild and cultivated, have been eaten since prehistoric times, their importance outside the monasteries, with the exception of the potato, has been secondary. Those that have been enjoyed are the easily grown vegetables such as turnips, carrots, parsnips, onions, cabbages and leeks, not forgeting the potato – the ubiquitous vegetable of Ireland.

Irish Farmhouse Bake

One of the most modern Irish dishes, combining the best traditional ingredients, potatoes, bacon, cream and cheese, to create a delicious and economical family dish.

50 g/2 oz butter

8 rashers smoked back bacon, cut in strips

1 large onion, finely chopped

125 g/4 oz mushrooms, sliced

6 potatoes, boiled

1 tablespoon chopped parsley

150 ml/¼ pint double cream

125 g/4 oz farmhouse Cheddar cheese, grated

salt and pepper

Melt half the butter in a pan and fry the bacon until cooked and beginning to brown. Remove from the pan and fry the onion and mushrooms until cooked and beginning to colour. Cut the potatoes into wedges and arrange with the fried bacon, mushrooms and onions in an oval 750—900 ml/1¼—1½ pint ovenproof dish. Season with salt and pepper and add the parsley. Pour over the cream and cover with the grated cheese. Bake in the preheated oven for 20–30 minutes until crisp and golden on top and very hot. Serve on its own or with grilled tomatoes.

COOK'S NOTES

A few wild mushrooms added to this dish make it very special.

Other vegetables such as sliced courgettes, cooked broccoli florets or cauliflower can be used as alternatives to the mushrooms. Irish smoked cheese and bacon can also give variety and flavour.

Serves 4
Preparation time: 30 minutes
Cooking time: 20–30 minutes
Oven temperature: 180°C (350°F), Gas Mark 4

Mixed Mushroom Frigasse

75 g/3 oz butter

1 onion, finely chopped

1 clove garlic, crushed

875 g/1¾ lb mushrooms of your choice, cleaned and sliced if large

1 teaspoon finely chopped marjoram

1 tablespoon finely chopped parsley

150 ml/¼ pint red wine

1 egg yolk

1 teaspoon cornflour

2 tablespoons cream

salt and pepper

For serving:

8 slices bread

2 tablespoons finely chopped parsley

Melt 50 g/2 oz of the butter in a large frying pan and fry the onion and garlic until soft but not coloured. Add the prepared mushrooms and continue to cook over a gentle heat for about 10 minutes to draw out their juices. The mushrooms should stew rather than fry. Add the marjoram, parsley and red wine and season with salt and pepper. Bring to the boil.

Blend the egg yolk with the cornflour and cream and use to thicken the wine and mushroom juices. Keep warm.

Toast the bread and cut a circle from each slice using an 8 cm/3½ inch cutter. Lay the circles of hot toast overlapping on 4 individual plates and divide the frigasse between each, piling them on the bread. Sprinkle with parsley and serve immediately.

COOK'S NOTES
Any variety of cultivated or wild mushroom can be used for this dish or one type only, depending on taste and availability.

The frigasse is also delicious with finger strips of fried bacon stirred in just before serving. Smaller portions make an excellent starter.

Serves 4 as a main course or 8 as a starter
Preparation time: 15–20 minutes
Cooking time: 20–25 minutes

Savoury Stuffed Potato Cakes

Heat the oil in a pan and fry the onion and bacon until beginning to colour. Add the mushrooms and continue to fry until they too begin to colour. Stir in the tomato and parsley and season with salt and pepper. Leave to go cold.

Prepare the Potato Bread dough, see page 129, but roll out slightly thinner and cut into 16 circles using a 7 cm/3 inch cutter. Moisten the edges of half the circles with a little water. Divide the filling between these leaving a small rim around the edge. Use the remaining circles to cover the filling, pressing the edges together to seal. Heat a frying pan with a little oil or butter, add the potato cakes and cook until brown on both sides and warmed through. This will take about 8–10 minutes. Serve with salad and pickled beetroot.

COOK'S NOTES

Any cooked vegetables can be used for the filling along with chopped cooked ham, smoked or poached salmon or smoked mackerel. Sometimes I use all vegetables for the filling and serve fried or grilled bacon and tomatoes on the side.

Serves 4
Preparation time: 30 minutes
Cooking time: 8–10 minutes

1 tablespoon oil

1 small onion, finely chopped

4 rashers bacon, derinded and diced

125 g/4 oz mushrooms, finely chopped

1 tomato, finely chopped

1 tablespoon finely chopped parsley

2 quantities Potato Bread dough, see page 129

oil or butter for frying

salt and pepper

Roasted Root Vegetables

500 g/1 lb carrots, peeled

500 g/1 lb parsnips, peeled

500 g/1 lb turnips, peeled

1 tablespoon oil

2 tablespoons honey

Cut the vegetables into 1 cm/½ inch cubes. Heat the oil in the pan and quickly fry the vegetables until just coloured. Transfer to a roasting dish, drizzle over the honey, toss to coat evenly and roast in the preheated oven for 1–1¼ hours, until tender and well glazed. Toss frequently during the cooking to prevent the honey from burning.

Serve with roast meat, poultry and game.

Serves 6
Preparation time: 15 minutes
Cooking time: 1–1¼ hours
Oven temperature: 200°C (400°F), Gas Mark 6

Parsnip Cakes

One of my grandmother's favourite recipes, made from the fresh parsnips grown in her cottage garden. The puréed flesh is mixed with flour and seasoning, dipped in egg and breadcrumbs and fried in hot oil or bacon fat.

Put the parsnips, flour, butter, mace and nutmeg in a large bowl, season with salt and pepper and beat well to combine. Divide into 4 pieces and mould each piece into a round flat cake, about 9.5 cm /3½ inches in diameter and 1–2 cm/½–¾ inch deep. Cut each cake in half.

Dip each cake into the beaten egg, toss in breadcrumbs, pressing them well into the cakes to give an even coating and fry in a little hot oil for 3–4 minutes on each side until cooked through and an even golden colour. Drain on absorbent kitchen paper and serve as a main course or an accompanying vegetable. Parsnip Cakes are particularly good served with pork, ham and roast beef as well as fried sausages and bacon.

COOK'S NOTES
Any root vegetable suitable for mashing such as carrots, potatoes and turnips can be used for this recipe, either on their own or in combinations. Different spices and herbs can also be added to give variety. The cakes can be shaped into small logs or croquettes and deep fried.

Makes 8 cakes
Preparation time: 20–30 minutes
Cooking time: 6–8 minutes

500 g/1 lb parsnips, cooked and mashed

6 tablespoons plain flour

5 g/¼ oz butter, melted

pinch ground mace

pinch ground nutmeg

1 egg, beaten

125–175 g/4–6 oz fresh breadcrumbs

oil, for frying

salt and pepper

Fried Turnip & Bacon

1 large turnip,
approximately 1.75 kg/
3½ lb in weight, peeled and
cubed

25 g/1 oz butter

8 rashers bacon, derinded

salt and pepper

Boil the turnip in a little water until tender, drain well and mash with half the butter until smooth. Season well with salt and pepper. Heat the remaining butter in a pan and fry the bacon until cooked and beginning to crisp. Remove from the pan and keep warm. Toss the mashed turnip in the bacon fat in the pan until all the flavour has been imparted then serve with the rashers of bacon and boiled potatoes in their jackets.

COOK'S NOTES

This is very much a country dish, perhaps not the most elegant in appearance but delicious in flavour. Fried sausages are sometimes used instead of the bacon.

Serves 4
Preparation time: 15 minutes
Cooking time: 20 minutes

There was an old woman,

Who lived in a lamp,

She had not room,

To beetle her champ.

(Traditional Rhyme)

Champ

*Champ, also known as cally, poundies and pandy, is one of the
most famous ways of serving Ireland's best loved vegetable – the
potato. Champ is this country's way of serving mashed potatoes.*

Heat a pan of salted water and boil the potatoes in their skins
until tender. Drain and dry over a low heat covered with a piece
of absorbent kitchen paper. Peel and mash well.

While the potatoes are cooking, put the milk and chopped
spring onions into a saucepan, bring to the boil and simmer for a
few minutes. Gradually beat into the mashed potatoes to form a
soft but not sloppy mixture. Beat in half the butter and season
with salt and pepper. Divide between 4 warm plates or bowls,
make a well in the centre of each serving, cut the remaining
butter into 4 pieces and put one piece in each of the hollows.
Serve immediately.

1 kg/2 lb potatoes,
unpeeled

150 ml/¼ pint milk

4–5 spring onions, finely
chopped

50–125 g/2–4 oz butter

salt and pepper

COOK'S NOTES

*Traditionally, champ would have been served as a main meal,
with a glass of milk or buttermilk. Nowadays, however, it is used
to accompany meats such as boiled ham and grilled sausages.
Parsley, young nettle tops, peas and broad beans can be
substituted for the spring onions.*

Serves 4

Preparation time: 5 minutes
Cooking time: 20–25 minutes

She up's with her beetle,

And broke the lamp,

And then she had room,

To beetle her champ.

(TRADITIONAL RHYME)

Colcannon

Similar to Champ, but flavoured, coloured and textured by the addition of cooked and shredded kale – a member of the cabbage family. Traditionally served at Hallowe'en.

500 g/1 lb kale or green leaf cabbage, stalk removed and finely shredded

500 g/1 lb potatoes, unpeeled

6 spring onions or chives, finely chopped

150 ml/¼ pint milk or cream

125 g/4 oz butter

salt and pepper

Heat a pan of salted water and boil the kale or cabbage in boiling water until very tender. This will take 10–20 minutes. At the same time heat another pan of salted water and boil the potatoes until tender. Place the spring onions and the milk or cream in a pan and simmer over a low heat for about 5 minutes.

Drain the kale or cabbage and mash. Drain the potatoes, peel and mash well. Add the hot milk and spring onions, beating well to give a soft fluffy texture. Beat in the kale or cabbage, season with salt and pepper and add half the butter. The colcannon should be a speckled, green colour. Heat through thoroughly before serving in individual dishes or bowls. Make a well in the centre of each serving and put a knob of the remaining butter in each. Serve immediately.

Colcannon, like champ, can be served as a main dish with a glass of buttermilk or as an accompanying vegetable.

COOK'S NOTES
Sometimes I blend the kale in a food processor along with the hot milk and spring onions before adding to the potatoes. This produces an even texture and overall green colour and makes an interesting alternative.

Serves 4–6
Preparation time: 15 minutes
Cooking time: 20 minutes

Did you ever eat Colcannon,

When 'twas made with yellow cream?

(TRADITIONAL RHYME)

puddings & desserts

Ireland has often been described as the land of milk and honey because of the variety and quality of her produce; milk, bread and honey being available in abundance. These, together with eggs, formed the basis of many of Ireland's traditional puddings and desserts, such as custards, baked puddings, and moulds. Wild and cultivated fruits of all varieties were also used and eaten, either on their own, with honey and cream, or made into fruit fools, jelly creams and pastry pies.

Bramble Mousse

A favourite autumn dessert, made from plump wild blackberries, puréed and mixed with cream and egg whites, to make a rich, well flavoured mousse.

500 g/1 lb prepared blackberries

75–125 g/3–4 oz caster sugar

juice of 1 lemon

15 g/½ oz powdered gelatine

150 ml/¼ pint whipping cream, lightly whipped

2 egg whites

For the decoration:

150 ml/¼ pint double cream, whipped

6–8 whole blackberries

Put the blackberries, sugar and lemon juice into a saucepan and simmer gently for 10 minutes. Press through a nylon sieve into a large mixing bowl. Put the gelatine and 4 tablespoons water in a small heatproof bowl and soak for a few minutes. Stand the bowl in a saucepan of hot water and stir the gelatine slowly to dissolve. Pour into the blackberry purée, whisking continually. When the mixture is beginning to set, fold in the cream.

Whisk the egg whites until they hold their shape then fold into the mousse mixture. Pour into 6–8 individual serving dishes and chill until set. Decorate each serving with a rosette of cream and a whole blackberry.

COOK'S NOTES
Gooseberries, rhubarb, blackcurrants and raspberries can all be used as an alternative to the blackberries, sweetening to taste. The fruit can be made into a purée, and frozen until required.

Serves 6–8
Preparation time: 30 minutes

Irish Whiskey Syllabub

rind and juice of 1 large lemon

6 tablespoons clear honey

8 tablespoons Irish malt whiskey

300 ml/½ pint double cream, chilled

grated nutmeg, to decorate

Put the lemon rind and juice, honey and whiskey into a large bowl and leave to stand for as long as possible to develop the flavours. Gradually whisk in the cream until the mixture begins to thicken. Spoon into wine glasses and chill until required.

If the syllabub is left for several hours, it will separate into a thick cream on top and a clear liquid at the bottom. Whether served immediately as a thick creamy concoction or after a few hours as a two layered delight, the syllabub should be decorated with nutmeg and served with Shortbread Fingers (see page 134).

Serves 4–6
Preparation time: 15 minutes

Gooseberry & Elderflower Fool

1 kg/2 lb green gooseberries, topped and tailed

2–3 sprigs elderflowers (optional)

175 g/6 oz caster sugar

300 ml/½ pint double cream, whipped until thick and holding its shape

fresh elderflowers, to decorate

Put the gooseberries, 65 ml/2½ fl oz water and the elderflowers, if using, into a saucepan and simmer gently until the fruit is soft. Remove the elderflowers and turn the fruit into a sieve to remove the excess juice. Put the fruit into a bowl and beat with a fork to form a purée. Stir in enough sugar to sweeten.

Tip the cream onto the gooseberry purée and fold carefully to combine. Spoon into 4 small glasses or dishes and chill well. Decorate with elderflowers and serve with sponge fingers or Shortbread Fingers (see page 134).

Serves 4–6
Preparation time: 20–30 minutes

Rich Shortcrust Pastry

*Halve the quantities of flour, butter and white fat and use
1 teaspoon caster sugar, 1 egg yolk and 2 teaspoons cold water to
give 125 g/4 oz pastry, which will line a 20 cm/8 inch flan tin.*

Sieve the flour and salt into a large mixing bowl, then cut the
butter and white fat into the flour and rub in until the mixture
resembles fine breadcrumbs. Stir in the sugar. Mix the egg yolk
with 3–4 tablespoons water and sprinkle over the top of the
crumbled mixture. Mix with a broad-bladed knife to form a stiff
dough. Work only long enough to form a ball. Leave the pastry to
rest in the refrigerator for about 30 minutes before using.

COOK'S NOTES

*The food processor is a most convenient way to make shortcrust
pastry and gives excellent results. Success however, depends on
careful processing to ensure that the dough is not overworked.*

*Pastry freezes well and can therefore be prepared in
advance.*

Makes pastry for 1 x 20 cm/8 inch double-crust tart

Preparation time: 15 minutes
Cooking time: see individual recipes
Oven temperature: between 180°C (350°F), Gas Mark 4 to
200°C (400°F), Gas Mark 6, see individual recipes

250 g/8 oz plain flour

pinch salt

125 g/4 oz butter or hard
margarine

50 g/2 oz hard white fat

1 tablespoon caster sugar

1 egg yolk

Irish Apple Pie

For the filling:

1.5–1.75 kg/3–3½ lb Bramley cooking apples, peeled, cored and thinly sliced

5 tablespoons granulated sugar

6 whole cloves

caster sugar, for sprinkling

For the pastry:

300 g/10 oz plain flour

pinch salt

150 g/5 oz butter or hard margarine

75 g/3 oz hard white fat

1 tablespoon caster sugar

1 egg yolk

4–5 tablespoons cold water

Prepare the pastry, see page 109. Divide into two and roll one piece 4 cm/1½ inches larger than an ovenproof pie plate. Line the plate with the pastry, cutting off the excess. Brush the pastry rim with lightly beaten egg white (reserved from making the pastry) and lay the pastry trimmings on top.

Arrange alternate layers of apples and sugar in the centre of the plate with the cloves. Roll out the second piece of pastry just large enough to cover the pie. Brush the pastry rim with egg white and cover the pie with the pastry lid. Press the edges firmly together to seal and flute to decorate. Brush the pie with the remaining egg white and sprinkle with caster sugar. Bake in the preheated oven for 10 minutes, then reduce the temperature and bake for a further 20–30 minutes, until the apples are just tender and the pastry pale gold in colour. Sprinkle with more caster sugar and serve hot or cold with whipped cream.

COOK'S NOTES

For Rhubarb Tart, use 1–1.5 kg/2–3 lb rhubarb, cut in 2 cm/ ¾ inch lengths, tossed in 2 tablespoons cornflour.

For Apple and Blackberry Pie, use 1 kg/2 lb cooking apples and 500 g/1 lb blackberries.

Serves 6–8
Preparation time: 30 minutes
Cooking time: 30–40 minutes
Oven temperature: 200°C (400°F), Gas Mark 6 for 10 minutes, then reduce the temperature to 180°C (350°F), Gas Mark 4 for a further 20–30 minutes

Treacle Tart

One of the many dessert dishes which found their way to Ireland, via the Anglo-Irish and are now much enjoyed throughout the country.

125 g/4 oz Rich Shortcrust Pastry, see page 109

For the filling:

175 g/6 oz fresh white breadcrumbs

325 g/11 oz golden syrup

grated rind of 1 lemon

approximately 50 ml/2 fl oz lemon juice

Roll out the pastry thinly on a floured surface and use to line a 20 cm/8 inch fluted flan ring or loose bottomed flan tin, about 4 cm/1½ inches deep. Mix together the ingredients for the filling and pour into the pastry case. Bake in the preheated oven for 20–30 minutes until the pastry is cooked and golden in colour. Serve hot or cold with lightly whipped cream.

Serves 6–8
Preparation time: 20–30 minutes
Cooking time: 20–30 minutes
Oven temperature: 190°C (375°F), Gas Mark 5

Irish Coffee

Warm a stemmed whiskey glass or Paris goblet with hot water. Put the sugar in the bottom of the glass and add very hot coffee to come to within 5 cm/2 inches from the top of the glass. Stir to dissolve the sugar. Add the whiskey.

Hold a teaspoon, curved side up, across the glass, barely touching the coffee and pour the cream from a jug very slowly over the spoon so that it floats on top of the coffee. The cream should be suspended on top of the whiskey laced coffee (it hasn't worked if it falls to the bottom). Serve after a meal or as a pick-me-up or as an excuse to celebrate.

Serves 1
Preparation time: 5 minutes

1 heaped teaspoon demerara sugar

1 cup of strong black coffee

approximately 1 double measure of Irish whiskey (75 ml/3 fl oz)

1–2 tablespoons chilled thick double cream

Irish Whiskey Trifle

Cut the Swiss roll into 1 cm/½ inch slices and arrange in a 1.2 litre/2 pint glass bowl. Sprinkle the whiskey over the sponge and top with the raspberries, reserving a few for decoration. Leave to soak while preparing the custard.

Place the cream in a saucepan and gently bring to simmering point. Beat the egg yolks, caster sugar and cornflour together until pale in colour. Pour on the cream, stirring continuously. Return the custard to the saucepan and cook over a low heat until thick, stirring constantly. Cool slightly before pouring over the trifle.

When cold spread the whipped cream on top of the custard and decorate with the remaining raspberries.

COOK'S NOTES
Trifle has many variations based on individual families' preferences. This basic trifle can be varied by using 300 ml/½ pint custard made with custard powder instead of homemade custard and a tin of mixed fruit instead of the raspberries. A fruit jelly can also be used to moisten the sponge and the fruit.

Serves 6–8
Preparation time: 30–40 minutes

1 x 500 g/1 lb Swiss roll, preferably homemade, filled with raspberry jam

50 ml/2 fl oz Irish whiskey

250 g/8 oz frozen raspberries

300 ml/½ pint double cream, whipped to hold its shape, to decorate

For the custard:

300 ml/½ pint double cream

3 egg yolks

25 g/1 oz caster sugar

1 teaspoon cornflour

Irish Cheese Plate with Spiced Fruit Compote

450 ml/¾ pint red wine

150 ml/¼ pint pure orange juice

grated rind and juice of 1 lemon

5 cm/2 inch stick cinnamon

6 whole peppercorns

6 whole allspice berries

1 blade of mace

375 g/12 oz mixed dried fruit (apricot, peaches, prunes, pears, dates, bananas or figs)

For the cheese plate:

a selection of 5–8 Irish cheeses, see Cook's Notes. Allow approximately 75 g/3 oz of cheese per person

watercress leaves, to garnish

Irish oat cakes, to serve

Combine the red wine, orange juice, water and lemon rind and juice in a large saucepan. Tie the spices in a piece of muslin and add to the pan. Bring to the boil, add the fruit and simmer gently for 30–40 minutes until the fruit is pulpy and tender. Leave to go cold.

Cut the cheese into similar sized triangles and arrange on large individual plates, spoon a little of the spiced compote on the side, garnish with watercress leaves and serve with Irish Oat Cakes (see page 126).

COOK'S NOTES

Irish Cheeses:
Cashel Blue: Semi-soft blue
Rathgore: Blue veined goats' cheese, similar to Roquefort
Milleens: Soft Camembert type
Cooleeney: Soft Camembert type

St Tola: Goats' cheese, log
Gubbeens: Semi-soft with unique flavour
Gubbeens: Semi-hard smoked
Fivemiletown: Oak smoked
Gabriel: Gruyère type
Irish Desmond: Hard, close textured
Lavistown: Semi-hard, Cheshire type
Ring: Irish Farmhouse Cheddar type

Serves 4
Preparation time: 20 minutes
Cooking time: 30–40 minutes for the compote

Brown Bread & Irish Whiskey Ice Cream

Combine the breadcrumbs and demerara sugar in a mixing bowl. Spread over a large roasting tray and bake in the preheated oven until the sugar has caramelized, this will take about 10 minutes. Leave to go cold.

Whisk the eggs and caster sugar until very thick, and pale cream in colour. Fold the caramelized bread into the eggs followed by the whiskey and double cream, whisked until it is just holding its shape. Pour into a rigid container and freeze overnight.

Serve two scoops of ice cream per person, decorated with a mint leaf and accompanied by Shortbread Fingers (see page 134).

COOK'S NOTES

Irish wheaten bread is not suitable for this ice cream as it makes it rather heavy and unappetising. However, any type of brown or granary bread is excellent.

Freezing is done in the deep freeze with no stirring or churning required. An ice cream maker is not needed.

Serves 9–10
Preparation time: 30 minutes, plus freezing overnight
Cooking time: 10 minutes, for the crumbs
Oven temperature: 240°C (475°F), Gas Mark 9

175 g/6 oz brown bread crumbs (not wheaten)

125 g/4 oz demerara sugar

3 eggs

65 g/2½ oz caster sugar

75 ml/3 fl oz Irish whiskey

450 ml/¾ pint double cream

fresh mint leaves, to decorate

I'll have none of your boxty,

I'll have none of your blarney,

But I'll whirl my petticoats over my head

And be off with my Royal Charlie.

(TRADITIONAL RHYME)

St Brendan's Cream

125 ml/4 fl oz St Brendan's or Bailey's Irish Cream liqueur

50 ml/2 fl oz sweet white wine

2 tablespoons lemon juice

50 g/2 oz caster sugar

300 ml/½ pint double cream

thin slices of lemon, to decorate

Combine the liqueur, wine, lemon juice and sugar in a bowl and whisk with an electric mixer to dissolve the sugar. Gradually add the cream, whisking all the time until the liquid begins to thicken. The mixture will look slightly curdled at first but will improve in texture as the whisking continues. When the mixture is holding its shape, spoon into long stemmed glasses. Chill for several hours, to develop the flavours, before serving. Decorate with lemon slices.

Serves 6
Preparation time: 15 minutes

Carrageen Moss Blancmange

40 g/1½ oz dried carrageen moss

finely grated rind of 1 lemon

900 ml/1½ pints milk

1 egg, size 2, separated

2–3 tablespoons caster sugar

Put the carrageen moss, lemon rind and milk into a pan and slowly bring to the boil. Simmer gently for 15–20 minutes until the carrageen swells and exudes jelly. Whisk the egg yolk and caster sugar together until pale in colour and pour on the carrageen mixture, rubbing all the jelly through a sieve. Stir to combine. Return to a clean pan, bring to the boil and cook over a gentle heat until the mixture coats the back of a wooden spoon. Leave to go cold. Whisk the egg white until stiff and gently fold into the cold carrageen mixture. Pour into a 900 ml/ 1½ pint wetted mould or 6 x 150 ml/¼ pint individual moulds or dishes. Refrigerate until set. Turn out of the mould and serve chilled with lightly stewed fruit or fresh berry fruits.

COOK'S NOTES
Carrageen is an edible seaweed also known as 'Irish Moss' or 'Sea Moss'. It is a rich source of agar jelly and is used for thickening both sweet and savoury dishes.

Serves 4–6
Preparation time: 10 minutes, plus cooling and setting

Bramley Apple Cheesecake

Stir the melted butter into the biscuit crumbs, press into the bottom of a lightly oiled 20 cm/8 inch loose bottomed cake tin about 5 cm/2 inches deep.

Stew the apples with the lemon juice and 1 tablespoon of water until soft. Stir in the sugar and egg yolks and leave to go cold. Add the cheese and liquidize until smooth. Pour into a large bowl. Dissolve the gelatine in 3 tablespoons of water and add to the apple mixture. Lightly whisk the egg whites and fold into the apple mixture with the cream and pour into the tin. Refrigerate overnight until set. Remove from the tin and decorate with rosettes of cream and apple slices.

COOK'S NOTES

This cheesecake is also excellent made with ricotta cheese. Soaking the apple slices for the decoration in a little lemon juice prevents them from discolouring.

Serves 8–10
Preparation time: 30 minutes, plus overnight refrigeration

50 g/2 oz unsalted butter, melted

150 g/5 oz digestive biscuits, crushed

For the filling:

1 kg/2 lb Bramley apples, peeled, cored and sliced

1 tablespoon lemon juice

75 g/3 oz caster sugar

2 eggs, size 2, separated

250 g/8 oz cream cheese

15 g/½ oz powdered gelatine

250 ml/8 fl oz cream, lightly whipped

For the decoration:

150 ml/¼ pint double cream, whipped

red-skinned apple, thinly sliced

Irish Curd Cheesecake

This is an eighteenth century dessert, adapted from the recipe manuscript of Lady Rivers, County Cavan, 1750.

125 g/4 oz Rich Shortcrust Pastry, see page 109

icing sugar, for dusting

For the filling:

50 g/2 oz softened butter

50 g/2 oz caster sugar

rind of 1 large lemon

juice of ½ lemon

pinch ground cinnamon

3 eggs, size 2, separated

3 tablespoons plain flour

375 g/12 oz cottage cheese, sieved

For the topping:

1 egg, size 2

1 tablespoon caster sugar

25 g/1 oz butter, melted

1 tablespoon plain flour

Roll out the pastry until about 3–4 mm/⅛ inch thick and use to line a 20 cm/8 inch loose-bottomed metal flan tin. Set the tin on a baking sheet.

Cream the butter and sugar together until light and fluffy, then beat in the lemon rind and juice, cinnamon, egg yolks and flour. Beat the egg whites until stiff and fold into the mixture. Pour into the pastry case.

Combine all the ingredients for the topping and pour on top of the filling. Bake in the preheated oven for 1–1¼ hours until the cake is golden in colour, risen and firm to the touch. Leave to cool in the tin before removing. Sprinkle with icing sugar and serve with cream or natural yogurt.

COOK'S NOTES
This was a very popular cake and dessert in Ireland during the eighteenth century, often flavoured with a favoured drink of the time, sherry. Sometimes rosewater would also have been used and the filling varied by the addition of 50–125 g/2–4 oz dried fruit.

Serves 6–8
Preparation time: 30 minutes
Cooking time: 1–1¼ hours
Oven temperature: 160°C (325°F), Gas Mark 3

breads &
cakes

The making of bread in its many different forms is one of the great traditions of the Irish kitchen. Bread is made with both bleached and whole-grain flour, flavoured with treacle and fruit and raised with buttermilk – the milk left over after the butter is removed from the churn. These breads, lovingly referred to as white and brown soda, are baked either on the griddle, or in the oven. Although bread is the cornerstone of the Irish baking tradition, the country is equally well known for its cakes of all shapes and sizes along, with its biscuits, tarts and sweets.

Currant Soda

500 g/1 lb soda bread flour

1 heaped teaspoon
bicarbonate of soda

pinch salt

50 g/2 oz caster sugar

125 g/4 oz dried fruit

400–475 ml/14–16 fl oz
buttermilk

15 g/½ oz butter

Sieve the flour and bicarbonate of soda into a large mixing bowl, then stir in the salt, sugar and fruit. Make a well in the centre and pour in almost all the buttermilk. Stir with a broad-bladed knife or wooden spoon to form a loose dough, adding the rest of the milk if necessary.

Use the butter to grease a 20 cm/8 inch round cake tin, approximately 7 cm/3 inches deep. Turn the dough into the tin leaving the surface rough. Sprinkle with a little flour, set the tin on a baking sheet and bake in the preheated oven for 30 minutes, then reduce the temperature and cook for a further 30 minutes until the bread is golden brown and crisp to the touch. A skewer inserted in the centre should come out clean. Remove from the oven, turn out of the tin and wrap in a clean cloth. When cold, cut in slices and serve buttered.

COOK'S NOTES

A savoury soda bannock can be made by adding cooked, chopped bacon, ham and herbs instead of the fruit, along with a strongly flavoured Cheddar type cheese.

Makes 1 round loaf

Preparation time: 10–15 minutes

Cooking time: 1–1¼ hours

Oven temperature: 200°C (400°F), Gas Mark 6 for 30 minutes, then reduce the temperature to 150°C (300°F), Gas Mark 2 for a further 30–40 minutes

Soda Farls

300 g/10 oz soda bread flour

1 teaspoon salt

250–300 ml/8–10 fl oz buttermilk

extra flour, for dusting

Sieve the flour and salt into a large bowl. (If using plain flour and raising agent, see Cook's Notes, sieve with the flour.) Make a well in the centre and add nearly all the buttermilk. Stir with a broad-bladed knife or wooden spoon to form a firm dough, adding the remaining milk if necessary.

Turn onto a lightly floured surface and knead lightly until a smooth ball is formed. Roll or pat out to form a circle approximately 21 cm/8½ inches in diameter and no more than 1 cm/½ inch thick. Cut into 4 farls or triangles.

Gently heat a griddle, heavy cast-iron or electric frying pan, sprinkle with a dusting of flour and when this begins to turn a pale beige colour, the temperature is correct for cooking. Set the farls on the pan and cook for about 6–10 minutes on each side until risen and pale beige in colour. When cooked, they will sound hollow when tapped.

Remove from the pan, wrap in a clean cloth until cool then cut in half, butter generously and eat immediately.

COOK'S NOTES

If soda bread flour is not available use plain flour plus ½ teaspoon of bicarbonate of soda and ½ teaspoon of cream of tartar.

Soda farls are an important feature of an Ulster Fry (see page 58) or as the container for holding a fried egg, bacon, sausage and potato bread for a quick but substantial snack called a 'sausage soda'.

Makes 4 farls

Preparation time: 10–15 minutes
Cooking time: 12–20 minutes

White Soda Bread

Sieve the flour, salt and bicarbonate of soda into a large mixing bowl and add the sugar to sweeten. Make a well in the centre and pour in almost all the buttermilk, stirring with a broad bladed knife or wooden spoon to mix to a spongy dough.

Use the butter to grease a 19 x 11 x 6 cm/7½ x 4½ x 2½ inch loaf tin and turn the porridge-like mixture into this, spreading it in the tin but leaving the surface rough. Sprinkle with a dusting of flour, place on a baking sheet and bake in the preheated oven for 30 minutes. After this time reduce the oven temperature and cook for a further 30 minutes until the bread is well risen, a light beige colour and crusty on top. Remove from the oven, and cover with a cloth. After 5 minutes, remove from the tin, wrap in the cloth and leave to cool before cutting. Serve cut in slices and buttered.

COOK'S NOTES

If soda bread flour is not available use plain flour plus 1 heaped teaspoon baking soda and 1 heaped teaspoon of cream of tartar.

All 'soda' style Irish breads need to be eaten the day they are baked or toasted or fried the second day.

Makes 1 x 1 kg/2 lb loaf
Preparation time: 10 minutes
Cooking time: 1 hour
Oven temperature: 200°C (400°F), Gas Mark 6 for 30 minutes, then reduce the temperature to 150°C (300°F), Gas Mark 2 for a further 30 minutes

500 g/1 lb soda bread flour

1 teaspoon salt

1 teaspoon bicarbonate of soda

25–50 g/1–2 oz caster sugar

400–475 ml/14–16 fl oz buttermilk

25 g/1 oz butter

Irish Oat Cakes

In Ireland, oats have always been an important and widely used food for making porridge, soup, coating fish and baking bread and biscuits. These simple, flat cakes would originally have been baked on a griddle, over a turf fire, or on a warmed hearth stone.

250 g/8 oz medium or fine oatmeal

50 g/2 oz plain flour

½ teaspoon bicarbonate of soda

¼ teaspoon cream of tartar

½ teaspoon salt

50 g/2 oz butter

extra oatmeal, for shaping

Put the oatmeal in a large bowl and sieve the flour, bicarbonate of soda, cream of tartar and salt on top. Make a well in the centre. Put 50 ml/2 fl oz hot water and the butter into a saucepan and bring to the boil. Pour into the well and mix to bind. Turn onto a work surface lightly scattered with oatmeal and roll into a round cake about 23 cm/9 inches in diameter and 3 mm/⅛ inch thick. Scatter more oatmeal on top of the cake and press it into the surface. Cut into 8 triangular cakes. Set on a floured baking sheet and bake in the preheated oven for about 40 minutes.

COOK'S NOTES
These traditional oat biscuits are delicious with butter, cheese and a glass of buttermilk.

They can also be cut into 7 cm/3 inch rounds and served as circular biscuits.

Makes 8 triangular cakes
Preparation time: 15 minutes
Cooking time: 40 minutes
Oven temperature: 180°C (350°F), Gas Mark 4

Griddle Scones

Combine the flour, sugar and fruit in a large mixing bowl. Make a well in the centre and pour in almost all the buttermilk. Stir with a wooden spoon or broad-bladed knife to form a firm dough, adding the remaining milk if necessary.

Turn the dough onto a lightly floured surface and knead very gently until a smooth ball is formed. Pat to a circle about 20 cm/ 8 inches in diameter and about 5 mm/¼ inch thick. Cut into 6 triangular shapes.

Gently heat a cast-iron griddle or heavy-bottomed frying pan, sprinkle with a little flour and when this begins to turn a pale beige colour, the temperature is correct for cooking. Set the scones on the pan and cook for 6–8 minutes on each side until risen and pale golden in colour. Serve hot or cold with butter and jam.

COOK'S NOTES
The scones can be made without the fruit and salt, and savoury items like fried chopped bacon, ham or herbs added for variety.

Makes 6 triangular scones
Preparation time: 10–15 minutes
Cooking time: 6–8 minutes

150 g/5 oz soda bread flour

1 teaspoon caster sugar

25 g/1 oz dried mixed fruit

125–150 ml/4–5 fl oz buttermilk

extra flour, for dusting

Irish Wheaten Bread

This particular bread is sometimes referred to as brown soda.

175 g/6 oz soda bread flour

1 teaspoon bicarbonate of soda

375 g/12 oz wholemeal flour

pinch salt

1–2 teaspoons brown sugar

400–475 ml/14–16 fl oz buttermilk

15 g/½ oz butter

Sieve the soda bread flour and bicarbonate of soda into a large mixing bowl, add the wholemeal flour, salt and sugar, stirring to blend. Make a well in the centre and pour in almost all the buttermilk, stirring with a broad-bladed knife or wooden spoon to form a loose dough.

Use the butter to grease a 19 x 11 x 6 cm/7½ x 4½ x 2½ inch loaf tin. Turn the dough into this leaving the surface rough. Sprinkle with a little extra wholemeal flour to give a nutty surface. Set on a baking sheet and bake in the preheated oven for 30 minutes, then reduce the temperature and continue to cook for a further 30 minutes until the bread is well risen, brown and crusty on top. When a skewer inserted into the centre comes out clean, the bread is cooked. Remove from the oven, turn out and wrap in a clean cloth and leave on a wire rack to go cold. Serve cut in slices and buttered.

COOK'S NOTES

Traditionally, good size breakfast cups would be used for measuring, with 1 cup of plain or soda bread flour being used to 2 cups of wholemeal flour and 1 cup of buttermilk.

The secret of good Irish bread is to mix quickly and lightly and not to overwork.

The texture of this bread can be varied depending on the coarseness of the wholemeal flour used.

Makes 1 x 1 kg/2 lb loaf

Preparation time: 10 minutes

Cooking time: 1 hour

Oven temperature: 200°C (400°F), Gas Mark 6 for 30 minutes, then reduce the temperature to 150°C (300°F), Gas Mark 2 for a further 30 minutes

Potato Bread

Put the potatoes into a large bowl and mix in the salt and butter. Stir in the flour to make a pliable dough. Turn onto a lightly floured surface and roll into a circular shape about 5 mm/¼ inch thick and 23 cm/9 inches in diameter. Cut into 6 farls (triangular shapes).

Potato bread is cooked on a cast-iron griddle or in a heavy-bottomed frying pan which is heated gently without fat or oil, only a light dusting of flour. When this begins to turn a pale beige colour the temperature is right for cooking. Arrange the farls on the pan and cook for about 2½ minutes on each side until lightly browned. Serve hot with butter and sugar or homemade jam. Alternatively, the bread after cooking may be fried and eaten with bacon, sausages and egg as part of an Ulster Fry (see page 58).

COOK'S NOTES

Potato bread is best made while the potatoes are still hot. If using leftovers, heat for 30 seconds in the microwave before mixing with the rest of the ingredients.

The potato bread can also be cut into 10 circles with a 7 cm/3 inch plain cutter.

Makes 6 farls

Preparation time: 5 minutes
Cooking time: 5 minutes

250 g/8 oz warm potatoes, cooked and mashed

½ teaspoon salt

25 g/1 oz butter, melted

50 g/2 oz plain flour, plus extra for dusting

Boxty Pancakes

A traditional potato dish, found in the northern counties of Cavan, Donegal, Leitrim and Monaghan. Boxty Pancakes are sometimes referred to as stamp.

500 g/1 lb potatoes, washed and peeled

2 tablespoons plain flour

1 teaspoon baking powder

salt and pepper

150 ml/¼ pint milk

oil, for frying

Grate the potatoes on a coarse grater into a bowl; add the flour sieved with the baking powder. Season with salt and pepper and mix in the milk. Drop tablespoons of this mixture on to a hot, lightly oiled pan or griddle. Cook for about 5 minutes on each side until golden brown. Serve hot with butter and sugar or fried bacon.

Makes 11 pancakes
Preparation time: 15 minutes
Cooking time: 30 minutes

Boxty on the griddle,

Boxty in the pan,

If you don't eat your boxty,

You'll never get a man.

Boxty on the griddle,

Boxty in the pan,

The wee one in the middle,

That one's for Mary Anne.

(TRADITIONAL RHYME)

Potato Apple Cake

This dish is the highlight of the farmhouse tea table, during the apple season, and also features in Hallowe'en festivities, when it is traditional for a ring to be hidden in the filling, to bring luck.

250 g/8 oz warm potatoes, cooked and mashed

½ teaspoon salt

25 g/1 oz butter

50 g/2 oz plain flour

caster sugar, to sweeten

50 g/2 oz butter, to finish

For the filling:

300 g/10 oz Bramley apples, peeled, cored and very thinly sliced

Prepare the Potato Bread dough (see page 129). Divide this in two and roll each piece to a 20 cm/8 inch circle. Divide the sliced apples between each circle piling them on one half only. Moisten the edge of the circle with a little water and fold the uncovered half of the potato bread on top of the apples to form a half moon shape. Press the edges together to seal.

Bake on a preheated griddle or pan for 15–20 minutes on each side to cook the apples and brown the bread. Just before serving, remove the cakes from the pan and set on a serving plate. Carefully open the cake along the curved edges, fold back the bread and sprinkle the apples with sugar and dot with butter. Seal the edges once more and put the cakes in a hot oven for 5–10 minutes to form a thick syrup. Serve immediately.

COOK'S NOTES

The Potato Apple Cake can also be eaten cold. In which case, a little sugar is added to the apples before cooking and the outside of the cake buttered before serving.

Makes 2 large cakes
Preparation time: 15 minutes
Cooking time: 45–50 minutes

Sponge Cake with Raspberry Jam and Fresh Cream

Grease 2 x 15 cm/6 inch sandwich tins and dust with a mixture of flour and caster sugar. Put the eggs and sugar in a large heatproof bowl, stand this over a pan of hot water and whisk until light and creamy. The mixture should be stiff enough to retain the impression of the whisk for a few seconds. This will take about 5–8 minutes. Remove from the heat and whisk until cold.

Sieve the flour and baking powder together and very lightly fold into the whisked mixture, one third at a time. Divide this between the two 15 cm/6 inch tins and bake near the top of the oven for 20 minutes. Leave in the tins until cold before turning out.

Sandwich the cakes together with the jam and cream and dust with sieved icing sugar.

COOK'S NOTES
For speed and convenience the eggs and sugar can be whisked in an electric mixer until thick and creamy. For a 20 cm/8 inch cake use 2 x 20 cm/8 inch tins, 4 eggs and cook for an extra 15 minutes.

Makes 1 x 15 cm/6 inch sponge cake
Preparation time: 15 minutes
Cooking time: 20 minutes
Oven temperature: 180°C (350°F), Gas Mark 4

3 eggs

125 g/4 oz caster sugar

75 g/3 oz plain flour

¼ teaspoon baking powder

3–4 tablespoons raspberry jam

150 ml/¼ pint double cream, whipped

icing sugar, to dust

Shortbread Fingers

These short, buttery biscuits are of Scottish origin and have been a feature of the Irish tea table for many years.

250 g/8 oz butter
125 g/4 oz caster sugar
50 g/2 oz cornflour
300 g/10 oz plain flour
caster sugar, for sprinkling

Cream the butter and sugar together until light and fluffy. Sieve in the cornflour and plain flour and mix well to combine. Press into an oblong tin approximately 30 x 20 cm/12 x 8 inches and mark with the prongs of a fork both ways. Bake in the preheated oven for 30 minutes, then reduce the temperature and cook for a further 1–1½ hours.

Remove from the oven and cut in to 32 even-size fingers. Sprinkle with caster sugar and leave to cool slightly in the tin before transferring to a cooling rack until firm. Store in an airtight tin.

COOK'S NOTES

The length of the cooking time will depend on how pale or dark in colour the biscuits are required. Alternatively, this mixture can also be rolled out thinly and cut into circular biscuits. Sometimes a little semolina is added to give a more crunchy texture.

Makes 32 fingers

Preparation time: 15 minutes
Cooking time: 1½–2 hours
Oven temperature: 140°C (275°F), Gas Mark 1 for 30 minutes, then reduce the temperature to 120°C (250°F), Gas Mark ½ for 1–1½ hours

Tea Brack

The word 'brack', in Irish breac, means speckled and refers to the fruit used in the dough. There are a number of different types of brack, this particular recipe is a cake rather than a bread and is moistened with tea.

275 g/9 oz sultanas

275 g/9 oz raisins

250 g/8 oz soft dark brown sugar

475 ml/16 fl oz strong black hot tea

15 g/½ oz butter, melted

375 g/12 oz plain flour

2 teaspoons baking powder

2 teaspoons mixed spice

2 eggs, size 2, beaten

Put the fruit and sugar into a large bowl and pour on the hot tea. Stir to dissolve the sugar, cover and leave overnight to allow the fruit to swell.

Line the bottom and sides of a 20 x 7 cm/8 x 3 inch round cake tin with greaseproof paper and grease lightly with the melted butter.

Sieve the flour, baking powder and spice together and mix into the fruit mixture alternately with the eggs, beating well between each addition. Pour into the prepared tin, smooth the top and bake in the preheated oven for approximately 1½ hours. Leave to cool in the tin before turning onto a wire rack. When cold store in an airtight tin.

Makes 1 x 20 x 7 cm/8 x 3 inch round cake

Preparation time: 15 minutes, plus overnight soaking

Cooking time: about 1½ hours

Oven temperature: 160°C (325°F), Gas Mark 3

Dropped Scones

Put the flour into a large mixing bowl with the sugar, make a well in the centre, break in the egg and beat with a wooden spoon to make a thick batter, gradually adding the buttermilk. Draw the flour from the sides of the bowl to the centre to prevent lumps from forming.

Slowly heat a cast-iron griddle or heavy-bottomed frying pan over a gentle heat. Grease lightly with a knob of butter wiping most of it off with kitchen paper. Drop the batter from the point of a tablespoon on to the pan. The scones will immediately begin to rise. When a few bubbles begin to break on the surface the scones are ready for turning. Turn them over gently and brown on the other side. When the scones are cooked they should be golden brown in colour and light and spongy in texture. Keep warm in a clean tea towel until they are all cooked, then serve with butter and jam.

COOK'S NOTES

If soda bread flour is not available, use 125 g/4 oz plain flour with 1 teaspoon bicarbonate of soda and 1 teaspoon cream of tartar.

These little dropped scones are traditionally served hot for afternoon tea.

Makes 14 scones

Preparation time: 5 minutes
Cooking time: 15 minutes

125 g/4 oz soda bread flour

25 g/1 oz caster sugar

1 egg, size 2

150 ml/¼ pint buttermilk

5 g/¼ oz butter, for greasing

Buttermilk Scones

250 g/8 oz plain flour, plus extra for dusting

1 teaspoon bicarbonate of soda

1 teaspoon cream of tartar

pinch of salt

25 g/1 oz butter

200 ml/7 fl oz buttermilk

beaten egg or milk, to glaze (optional)

Sieve the dry ingredients into a bowl. Cut the butter into small pieces and rub into the flour until the mixture resembles fine breadcrumbs. Make a well in the centre and add almost all the buttermilk, mixing with a wooden spoon or broad-bladed knife to form a soft dough. Turn onto a lightly floured work surface, knead very gently to form a round shape and roll out to about 2 cm/¾ inch thick. Cut into scones using a 5–6 cm/2–2½ inch cutter.

Place on a lightly floured baking sheet and brush with egg or milk to glaze. Bake in the preheated oven for 15–20 minutes until well risen and light golden in colour. Serve hot or cold with butter or jam.

COOK'S NOTES

For fruit scones add 25–50 g/1–2 oz dried fruit or cherries and 25–50 g/1–2 oz caster sugar before adding the milk.

For savoury scones add 50 g/2 oz grated cheese, some diced cooked bacon or herbs.

For wheaten scones use half wholemeal and half plain flour.

Makes 8–12 scones

Preparation time: 15 minutes
Cooking time: 15–20 minutes
Oven temperature: 220°C (425°F), Gas Mark 7

Boiled Fruit Cake

Fruit breads and cakes are an important feature of the Irish tea table. This boiled cake is richly flavoured with fruit and spice but is more economical than a more traditional rich fruit cake.

Put the butter, sugar, fruit and 250 ml/8 fl oz water into a large saucepan, bring to the boil, then reduce the temperature and simmer for 10 minutes. Leave to cool. Sieve the flour, baking powder, bicarbonate of soda and spice together and fold into the fruit mixture along with the almond essence and beaten eggs.

Pour into an 18 cm/7 inch deep cake tin, lined with greaseproof paper and well greased. Bake in the preheated oven for 1½ hours until risen and set. Leave to cool slightly in the tin before turning out and leaving to go completely cold. Wrap in greaseproof paper or foil and store in an airtight tin.

COOK'S NOTES

This cake is deliciously moist and perfect for afternoon tea served in slices, spread with butter.

The cake will always taste better if the tin has been greased with melted butter.

Makes 1 x 18 cm/7 inch cake
Preparation time: 20–30 minutes
Cooking time: 1½ hours
Oven temperature: 150°C (300°F), Gas Mark 2

50 g/5 oz butter

150 g/5 oz soft brown sugar

375 g/12 oz dried mixed fruit

250 g/8 oz plain flour

1 teaspoon baking powder

1 teaspoon bicarbonate of soda

2 teaspoons mixed spice

½ teaspoon almond essence

2 eggs, beaten

glossary

Bacon: the sides of the pig, known as the 'flitch', were cured as bacon. To cure the pig, the flesh was rubbed with a mixture of salt, sugar and saltpetre, up to two weeks before being dried. It was often hung by the fire to smoke over a mixture of turf and oak. Nowadays, most pork is cured in a salt solution.

Bairm Brack: the traditional bread eaten at Hallowe'en. The word *breac* means speckled and refers to the fruit used in the dough. Bairm, which is yeast, was used to leaven the cake or bread. Sometimes referred to as barm or barn brack. When eaten at Hallowe'en, the bread has 'rings' hidden in the dough, which signifies marriage before Easter for whoever is lucky enough to find one in their slice. Bairm Brack is also popular throughout the year as a tea-time cake.

Baking Soda: also known as bicarbonate of soda or sodium bicarbonate. Used as a raising agent in Irish breads, along with 'sour' milk.

Bannock: one of Ireland's most popular soda breads. The basic soda bread recipe being enriched with fruit. Traditionally cooked in a pot-oven, over a turf fire in the open hearth. It is served, cut in slices, with butter. Also known as fruit soda, currant soda and curranty cake.

Bard: a poet or singer.

Beastlings: the first new milk given by a newly calved cow.

Black Pudding: also known as blood pudding. Made from cow, sheep or pig blood, mixed with fat, milk or cream and cereal – generally oatmeal – herbs, spices and seasoning. In appearance, black puddings resemble very plump sausages.

Brigid (Brigit): the daughter of Dagda and the goddess of healing, smiths, fertility and poetry. Her festival, held on 1 February, was one of the four great festivals of the Celtic world. (see also St Brigid)

Broth: a substantial soup, flavoured with meat, enriched with pulses and root vegetables and thickened with cereal. The earliest broth was thickened with oats, giving it a porridge like texture. Nowadays, barley is more frequently used.

Brown Soda: soda bread made using wholegrain flour. (see also Soda Bread; Soda Bread Flour; White Soda)

Buttermilk: the milk left over, after cream has been churned into butter. One of the main ingredients used in the making of traditional Irish breads. Also highly prized as a drink and at one time, in country areas, served with almost every meal.

Buttermilk Plant: a plant-like structure composed of yeast and bacteria.

Byre: a cattle barn.

Carrageen: also known as sea moss and Irish moss. A branching viscous seaweed found on coastal rocks all over Ireland. A rich source of agar jelly, which is used for thickening and setting sweet and savoury dishes. It is sold dried in health food and specialist shops.

Cúchulainn: one of the most famous heroes of Irish mythology and reputedly the son of the god Lugh.

Curds: the by-product formed when milk is soured either naturally or by the addition of buttermilk or rennet. One of the most important foods for the Irish until the introduction of the potato in the seventeenth century. Eaten as they were or made into cheese.

Drisheen: the black pudding of county Cork. Made from sheep blood and flavoured with the herb tansy, its texture resembles that of a baked custard.

Druids: ministers of the Celtic religion, as well as philosophers, advisers, judges and teachers. Known throughout the Celtic world, not just in Ireland. In Irish mythology they featured mainly as masters of the supernatural arts and were both male and female.

Fadge: another name for potato bread, or potato cake, most commonly used in the thenorthern counties of Ireland.

Frigasse: also known as frigacy or fricassee. Frigasse was the word used in a number of eighteenth-century Irish manuscript 'receipt' books to describe a method of preparing poultry or game. The meat is cut into pieces, cooked by stewing or boiling, then served in a rich sauce, made from the cooking liquor, thickened with egg yolk and cream.

Gael: the son of Niul, the progenitor of the Gaelic people.

Ham: the hind legs of the pig, a prime cut, dry or wet, cured as for bacon.

Kale: a cabbage with open curled green leaves. Used for making colcannon.

Legend: a traditional story which may or may not be true.

Leaven: the ferment which makes dough rise. This may be produced by the use of yeast, bicarbonate of soda, bairn, buttermilk or sour milk.

Lugh: one of the most important of the gods of Ireland. A sun god and a god of the arts and crafts: the father of Cúchulainn.

Myth: an ancient traditional story of gods or heroes: a commonly held belief that is purely fictional.

Porter: a weak, dark coloured beer, with a bitter flavour, which is brewed from charred or browned malt.

Potato Farls: Also known as potato cakes or fadge. Circles of potato bread cut into triangular pieces called farls.

St Brigid: the Christian saint who takes second place only to St Patrick. Her traditions have associations with those of the goddess Brigid, as does her feast day, which takes place on the same date.

Saltpetre: potassium nitrate, a white crystalline salty substance used both to preserve meat and to give it a rich pinky-red colouring.

Scallions: another name for spring onions. The white and green parts are both used to flavour the milk which is used to make champ.

Scribe: an ancient or medieval official writer or copyist of manuscripts.

Soda Bread: made using brown, wholegrain or refined white flour, raised by using bicarbonate of soda with buttermilk. (see also Brown Soda; Soda Bread Flour)

Soda Bread Flour: a commercially prepared plain flour to which bicarbonate of soda is added. (see also Brown Soda; Soda Bread; White Soda)

Soda Farls: triangular pieces of bread made from the basic soda bread mixture, rolled into a circle and cut into pieces known as farls. Sometimes refered to as 'pointers'.

Stout: extra strong porter.

Sweet Milk: normal cows milk.

Tír-na-nog: Tír is the Irish word for land or country - Tír na-nog – Land of Youth, Country of the Young. Here one gains eternal youth.

Tuatha de Danaan: the race that inhabited Ireland before the arrival of the Milesians (the ancestors of the Gaels). They were the gods of the pre-Christian Irish.

White Pudding: similar to black pudding, but not made with blood. White pudding contains only oatmeal, lard, onion, herbs and seasoning.

White Soda: soda bread made using refined white flour. (see also Brown Soda; Soda Bread; Soda Bread Flour)

index

Bibliography
Ronan Coghlan, Irish Myth and
Legend, Appletree Press, Belfast
1985
Clare Connery, In an Irish
Country Kitchen, Weidenfeld &
Nicholson, London 1996
Kevin Danaher, The Year in
Ireland, Mercier Press, Cork &
Dublin 1972
Frank Delaney, The Celts, Harper
Collins, London 1993. Legends of
the Celts Harper Collins London
1994
Peter Berresford Ellis, A
Dictionary of Irish Mythology,
Oxford University Press, Oxford
1992
Evans, E, Estyn, Irish Folk Ways,
Routledge & Kegan Paul Ltd,
London 1957
Henry Glassie, Irish Folk History,
O'Brien Press, Dublin 1982
Maire MacNeill, The Festival of
Lughnasa, Oxford University
press, Oxford 1962
WB Yeats, The Book of Fairy and
Folk Tales of Ireland, Smithmark,
New York, 1996

Quotations
F Delaney, Legends of the Celts
p7
WB Yeats The Book of Fairy and
Folk Tales of Ireland p8
WB Yeats 'The Stolen Child', The
Collected Poems of WB Yeats p9
Permission from A.P. Watt Ltd on
behalf of Anne and Michael Yeats
Jonathan Swift, 'Onions' pages
14, 30 & 73, 'The Progress of
Poetry' p90
Anonymous traditional rhyme,
'Colcannon' pages 24, 46, 63 &
102
Anonymous traditional rhyme,
'Champ' pages 100 & 101
Anonymous traditional rhyme,
'Boxty' pages 115 & 130